BERLITZ®

D0796249

RIO DE JANEIRO

Berlitz Trademark Reg. U.S. Patent Office and other countries.
Marca Registrada.Library of Congress Catalog Card Number:
80-69545.

Printed in Switzerland by Weber S.A., Bienne

12th edition (1994/1995)

How to use our guide

- All the practical information, hints and tips that you will need before and during the trip start on page 102.
- For general background, see the sections Rio de Janeiro and the Cariocas, p. 6, and A Brief History, p. 12.
- All the sights to see are listed between pages 21 and 60, with suggestions on daytrips from Rio on pages 61 to 73. Our own choice of sights most highly recommended is pinpointed by the Berlitz symbol.
- Entertainment, nightlife and all other leisure activities are described between pages 74 and 92, while information on restaurants and cuisine is to be found on pages 92 to 101.
- Finally, there is an index at the back of the book, pp. 127–128.

Although we make every effort to ensure the accuracy of all the information in this book, changes occur incessantly. We cannot therefore take responsibility for facts, prices, addresses and circumstances in general that are constantly subject to alteration. If you have any new information, suggestions or corrections to contribute, we would be pleased to hear from you. Please write to Berlitz Publishing, Peterley Road, Oxford OX4 2TX, England.

Text: Ken Bernstein
Photography: Eric Jaquier; pp. 2–3 Françoise Witheridge
Layout: Hanspeter Schmidt
We are grateful to Cristina Silva, to Varig Airlines and to Tom Murphy for their help in the preparation of this book.
Cartography: Falk-Verlag, Hamburg.

Contents

Cover picture: View of Sugar Loaf

Rio de Janeiro and the Cariocas

Magnificent scenery, relaxed and hospitable people, the sound of the samba in the streets, glorious beaches… It's all true! What's more, Rio de Janeiro is one of the world's biggest tropical cities, superimposing all the metropolitan conveniences and excitements onto a happy scene of noble palms and blinding white sand.

Like all the wonders of the world, Rio ought to be examined from many perspectives. Study it from the ferryboat that crosses Guanabara Bay, a majestic harbor dappled with islands and surrounded by green hills. View it from the aerial cableway strung to the top of Sugar Loaf, with the yachts below like toy boats, and the gardens and beaches of Flamengo sprawling like an artist's conception of a futuristic urban plan. See it on foot, surrounded by historic churches and colonial palaces. Survey it from the towering statue of Christ the Redeemer that stands like a symbol above Rio, a city embraced by both mountains and sea.

Another good vantage point is the beach – perhaps the graceful arc of Copacabana or the stylish strand of Ipanema. On the shores

Storied Sugar Loaf presides over Rio's beaches and bay.

of the South Atlantic, soaking up the sun, you're closer than ever to the Cariocas, the people who call this city home.

The population of Rio de Janeiro is over seven million and multiplying fast. More than two million live in shantytowns that grow like mushrooms on the steep hillsides. These communities, called *favelas*, enjoy some fabulous vistas – better than the views from the penthouses of the millionaires below them. But poverty is no fun. For an escape, the poor join the rich on the world's most democratic beaches and in the annual bacchanal of Carnival. But every day, in spite of the problems, Rio is pervaded by a *joie de vivre* as warm and tangible as a summer drizzle.

Sometimes it seems half the population of Rio must be on honeymoon, what with all the public displays of affection and exchanges of passionate glances. While they're as romantic as Parisians, the Cariocas are also as animated as Romans and just as nocturnal as the night owls of Madrid. Like New Yorkers, they have a sly sense of humor to go with their big-city accent. Like Texans, they're certain they live in the best of all possible places, 7 and everywhere everyone is anxious to make sure you agree.

Rio is about as close to the equator as Havana, which means that winter is merely a formality. In July (the worst of winter south of the equator) the average temperature in Rio dips to only 69° Fahrenheit. This scarcely interferes with the outdoor way of life, which keeps the beaches crowded for most of the year.

In January, midsummer in Rio, the mean temperature averages about 78°F. But the statistics skim over all those afternoons, sometimes ten in a row, when the mercury boils up to 95°. So the change of climate, as much as the jet lag, is something of a shock after the journey from New York or London. It may take a day or two to get used to hiding under a beach umbrella in January.

It could take even longer to become immune to the sight of the beautiful Carioca women. To match their spectacular achievements, the young men devote a great deal of time to muscle-building endeavors and hectic sports. The beautiful people of Rio, even those whose skin is naturally the color of chocolate, smear on tanning lotion and bask in the noonday sun. This is one

resort city where the natives are just as keen on beach life as the tourists.

The original inhabitants of Brazil were Indians. In the 16th century the Portuguese colonized the country. They enslaved the Indians and established the Catholic religion and Portuguese language and culture in what is now South America's biggest nation.

When the sugar mills needed more manpower, black slaves were imported from Africa. The Portuguese were noted for their friendly, and in many cases affectionate, relations with their slaves. The eventual result was a multiracial population and, according to the anthropologist Gilberto Freyre. 'the unmistakable stamp of Negro influence' on all Brazilians regardless of color. Though racial harmony is more pronounced than in virtually any other country, Brazil's many-hued society makes no claims to perfection.

Brazilians of all races agree in their admiration of *mulatas*, girls with skin the color of *café-au-lait*, whose beauty, grace and

Itinerant salesmen let the aroma sell freshly fried popcorn.

sensuality contribute much to Rio's fame. Contemplating this voluptuous phenomenon, the eminent geographer Alberto Ribeiro Lamego was moved to write a paean: 'You are the essence of all the races... You come from afar, from an inscrutable past. From the white race, from the black and from the Indian. From Europe, Africa and Asia. You are the Universal Woman.'

Apart from women, the most obsessional interest of most Carioca men is soccer. You'll see this fanaticism in Maracanã Stadium at even the most routine match. And you'll see it on the beach on a day so torrid it's an effort just to flag down the soft-drink peddler. Barefoot in the scorching sand, teams of young footballers are running full tilt, maneuvering as nimbly as Fred Astaire, kicking as authoritatively as a cannon. Every year a few are 'discovered' and find fame and fortune; one or two in a lifetime will, like Pelé, become a national monument. Every boy can dream and come down from the *favela* to the wide open beach and practice his trick kick.

Everything else happens on the beach, too – so don't count on an undisturbed snooze. If you're not hit by a misplaced soccer ball, or by a volleyball or crashed kite, then you'll be kept awake by the cries of the ambulatory refreshment salesmen and the whine of a venerable biplane towing an advertising sign. At best the disturbance will be a youngster shaking a matchbox. That's all it takes to make the rhythm of the samba; the rest comes naturally. Even the most aloof foreigner can't resist a smile and a surreptitious tapping of the feet.

Thanks to the climate and the 'body beautiful' fixation of the Cariocas, much time and energy is devoted to outdoor sports. Early in the morning and at night, joggers will find plenty of company on the mosaic beachside pavements. Surfers and windsurfers fly through the waves, while hang-glider pilots execute lazy turns high above the sands.

Next to soccer, the biggest spectator sport is horse racing. Cariocas do a lot of betting, on and off the track. They also take the soccer pools very seriously. Failing that, they buy lottery tickets or take mildly illegal flutters in the *jogo do bicho* (animal game), a numbers racket appealing to hunch-players from many layers of society.

Reminder of indigenous culture: musicians from northeast Brazil playing at a Rio Sunday market.

Any time after November, you can take a glimpse behind the scenes of Carnival in Rio. As the weeks go by, excitement spreads to every neighborhood. The whole powderkeg of passions finally catches fire during the last five days before Lent, when everybody in town – including more tourists than can comfortably be accommodated – joins the round-the-clock spree. With its frenzy of music, color and happiness, Rio's annual extravaganza is, by any standards, one of life's overwhelming experiences.

Year-round, nightclubs in Rio feature amazing samba dancers. Some also present simulations of *macumba* religious rites imported from Africa. Forcibly converted to Christianity, the slaves quietly continued their old beliefs in parallel with the new; every saint had his or her pagan counterpart, so lighting a candle in church was not so different from burning one at a pagan ceremony. Seeing the authentic *umbanda* ritual takes **11** contacts and planning, but you'll notice the candles flickering on the beach at night. On New Year's Eve, thousands of believers flock to Copacabana and other beaches with offerings for the goddess of the sea. Even the most sophisticated Carioca probably has a *figa*, an amulet in the form of a fist with the thumb extended between the second and third fingers. Warding off the evil eye, it also ensures luck and fertility.

The 'thumbs up' sign of optimism is also typical of Rio. The customary greeting is *'Tudo bem?'* – like the French *'Ça va?'* or the American 'How's everything?' The answer is a hearty *'Tudo bem!'* – 'All's well!' – with a smile, and a thumb jabbed upward as an exclamation point.

In Rio smiles come easily in spite of the shocking rates of inflation and crime, the housing crisis, the helter-skelter traffic, and the oppressive parking problem. It's easy to be optimistic when you're awakened every morning by the twitter of tropical birds in the palm trees, when you live among such beautiful people and places. The Cariocas themselves call Rio *A Cidade Maravilhosa* the Marvelous City. They ought to know.

A Brief History

Pedro Álvares Cabral, a Portuguese explorer, discovered Brazil in 1500 – which is convenient for the generations of school children who have had to memorize the date. It was also fortuitous for the Portuguese empire that Cabral 'waited' until the Treaty of Tordesillas was in force. Under this 1494 pact, Portugal and Spain had grandly divided the presumed spoils of the New World by drawing a vertical line down the still empty map. The Brazilian coast neatly dropped into the eastern zone – reserved, sight unseen, for Portugal.

Cabral was not hugely impressed by his discovery. First, he mistakenly thought he had found an island, not the South American mainland. And, having hoped to exploit the riches of the Orient, he was frankly disappointed to meet with savages similar to the ones Columbus was calling Indians. They belonged to the Tupi-Guarani family of tribes and were later to intermarry with the predominantly male settlers, producing the beginnings of the racially mixed society that has come to characterize Brazil.

Expeditions which followed could report only one resource of commercial interest, the tree named *pau-brasil* (brazilwood). The country was thus named for the tree, and not the other way around. Brazil held rich agricultural promise, but its potential has never been fully developed, even to this day, due to a series of misguided attempts to speculate on one-crop agriculture – first sugar, then coffee and later rubber.

The naming of Rio de Janeiro was based on a misunderstanding. A popular version says the Portuguese navigator Gonçalo Coelho reached Guanabara Bay on January 1 of the year 1502. Mistakenly thinking the bay was the mouth of a river, the explorer looked at his calendar and proclaimed it the 'River of January' – Rio de Janeiro in Portuguese. A band of uncooperative scholars stubbornly insists that the date was actually April 30th; and the year is in dispute, too.

French Threats

Half a century passed before anyone thought of establishing a town on the beautiful bay. To the dismay of Lisbon, the pioneer was a French admiral, Nicolas Durand de Villegaignon. To the dismay of Rome, the French settlers included a detachment of Protestants. The twin challenges of what was provocatively named *la France Atlantique* spurred Portugal to military action, which went on intermittently for several years. The French were finally dislodged on January 20, 1567. This was the day of the Italian martyr St Sebastian, who became Rio's patron saint. Consequently the official name of the city is still São Sebastião do Rio de Janeiro. In the hour of victory, the leader of the Portuguese forces, Estácio de Sá, was mortally wounded by an arrow.

After the French fled, the Portuguese governor general, Mem de Sá, moved the centre of Rio life from the base of the spectacular Sugar Loaf mountain to a less vulnerable location on the hill known as Morro do Castelo. No sign of this hill exists today; it was bulldozed to provide landfill to extend the modern metropolis into the bay. Mem de Sá, who just happened to be the uncle of the martyred Estácio de Sá, appointed Salvador Corrêa de Sá to be captain of the colony. Salvador was also a nephew of Mem de Sá. Nepotism is still a familiar feature of Brazilian life. **13**

Mid-nineteenth-century view of Rio dockside area. During the long reign of Pedro II, Rio de Janeiro began its expansion as a capital.

In 1710 another French force put Rio on the alert. Half a dozen landing craft of the privateer Jean-François Duclerc beached far to the southwest at Guaratiba. More than a thousand French troops then advanced on Rio overland. The defending army, which had a healthy numerical advantage, repelled the invaders, who suffered terrible losses. Duclerc himself surrendered, only to be murdered while in captivity.

To avenge his assassinated comrade, the privateer René Duguay-Trouin attacked Rio the following year. Although his siz-

A. Held, Ecublens, Suisse

able flotilla was sighted approaching Guanabara Bay, the governor, Castro Morais, failed to organize a coherent defense plan. As a result, Rio was captured. According to the Brazilian chronicles, the French sacked the town and took in ransom what was left. Duguay-Trouin's fleet, now laden with booty, including 200 head of cattle, 100 crates of sugar and 1,000 cruzados, slipped away before Portuguese reinforcements could arrive. Governor Castro Morais was banished from the city for his bungling.

Capital City

The cultivation of sugar cane, and later the sensational discoveries of gold and diamonds, made Brazil an economically interesting proposition in the 17th and 18th centuries. African slaves were imported to work the cane fields. They mixed with the white and Indian population, adding to the racial diversity of the territory.

Brazil was duly elevated from the status of a colony to a viceroyalty, and in 1763 the capital was moved from Bahia to Rio de Janeiro, which was closer to the gold and diamonds. Rio was a small and easy-going tropical town, lacking much in the way of amenities. The first viceroy to take up residence, a fastidious nobleman, hastily moved house from what he considered the loathsome, swampy Guanabara bayfront to the relatively fresh air of nearby hills. Rio's role as a great cosmopolitan capital could hardly have been imagined until the new century changed the map of Europe. **15**

Napoleon was on the move, sealing the Continent from England. Portugal refused to fall into line, so Marshal Andoche Junot and his formidable army crossed through Spain and invaded, aiming for Lisbon. The Portuguese royal court made a quick decision to stage a strategic retreat – to a safe haven across the sea. It was as if the British royal family, plus Parliament and civil servants, had evacuated London during World War II to establish the imperial capital in Pretoria or Canberra. In 1807 Dom João of Portugal, who served as regent for his mother, the mentally ill Queen Maria I, chose Brazil.

After Portugal's liberation from Napoleon, Dom João decided to remain in Brazil; and when Mad Maria died in 1816, he was crowned king in Rio's Igreja do Carmo (Carmelite Church). João VI was a popular monarch, and during his reign Rio began to take on the appearance of a civilized city, with an academy of fine arts, a national museum, a botanical garden, a bank and a newspaper.

Brazilian Empire

In 1821 King João was induced to return to Lisbon and assume control of his country. He handed over Brazil to his eldest son, Dom Pedro, and his bride, the Archduchess Leopoldina Josepha Carolina of Habsburg, the daughter of the Emperor of Austria. Though Leopoldina was no beauty – Pedro had wed her by proxy on the basis of a flagrantly retouched portrait – she was a popular queen who produced the first Brazilian-born heir to the throne.

Relations between Portugal and Brazil deteriorated rapidly, and in 1822, with pressure building in Brazil for independence, King Pedro leaped aboard the bandwagon. Tearing Portuguese medals and emblems from his uniform, he declaimed, 'Independence or death!' He was crowned Emperor of Brazil. Three years later, thanks to heavy pressure from Austria and Britain, the Portuguese government officially acknowledged the independence of Brazil. When King João died in 1826, Pedro I of Brazil (João's son) assumed the additional title of Pedro IV of Portugal, which he passed on to his daughter.

But Pedro's Brazilian subjects were growing restless at his stubborn, autocratic rule. Faced with a military coup in 1831, he abdicated in favour of his five-year-old son, who became Pedro II.

The dethroned father sailed to Portugal to fight for the crown of the mother country, which he won for his daughter after a long and bitter civil war, only to die at the age of 36.

Golden Age

Pedro II was declared of age in 1840 and ruled for nearly half a century more, during which Rio de Janeiro prospered. Fish-oil lamps gave way to gaslight on the streets of the capital, and by 1872 the population had climbed to 275,000. Steamboats linked Rio and Paris – not to mention Rio and Niterói across the bay – and horse-drawn trams brought mass transportation to the metropolis. Matching this technological progress, the city's social growth was marked by the foundation of schools, colleges, institutes and hospitals.

Under Pedro's reign, traditional absolutism evolved into a parliamentary monarchy with a two-party system. In 1850 the slave trade was outlawed, but the emperor was determined to push his country to the total abolition of slavery. The end of the struggle came in 1888. At the time, Pedro was abroad, so the abolition law was signed by his daughter, acting as regent; consequently the princess was dubbed Isabel the Redeemer.

Fierce opposition from slave-owners was thus added to the smouldering dissatisfactions of feuding politicians and military men. The anti-monarchical pot finally boiled over in November, 1889. With the emperor at the summer palace in Petrópolis, plotters in Rio de Janeiro set in motion a bloodless coup. Pedro was forced to abdicate and the royal family was expelled from the country before counter revolutionary forces could rally round the crown. The victors proclaimed a federal republic, the United States of Brazil.

Twentieth-Century Rio

In the first decade of the 20th century, Rio de Janeiro began to take on the appearance of a modern capital city. A wide, straight main street, now called Avenida Rio Branco, was paved – though the city had but four automobiles in 1904. Two tunnels brought Copacabana within easier reach of the business district. The port of Rio was developed; immigration ran at about 100,000 a year. A crash program of sanitation eradicated outbreaks of yellow fever by 1907, when the capital's population stood at 800,000.

World War I proved a boon to the Brazilian economy. Exports to the Allies multiplied, and industry expanded to fill the gap in imports. German submarine activity brought to an end efforts to stay neutral; and having joined the winning side, Brazil benefited from postwar settlements.

The New York stock-market crash of 1929 sent shock waves as far as Rio. The bottom fell out of the coffee market, and the rest of Brazilian agriculture and industry suffered. It was a moment ripe for political turmoil. Plots and counterplots were being hatched, and finally a revolution overthrew the government. A junta of military officers based in Rio gave power to a tough politician from the Gaucho country of Rio Grande do Sul, Getúlio Vargas.

In 1937, Vargas inaugurated the *Estado Novo* (New State), in-

Rio is an architectural melting pot where old and new coexist.

18

volving a continuous state of emergency, censorship and – for serious offenses like assassinating the president – the revival of the death penalty. A decree that photographs of the dictator had to be displayed in public places, including business premises, set the tone for his administration.

Under the Vargas regime, Brazil joined the Allies in World War II, as it had done in the previous 'War to End All Wars'.

Brazilian troops arrived in Italy in 1944 and won battles and commendations. At the end of the war, Vargas was ousted in a coup; but he returned in triumph in the election of 1950. Political commentators found him less effective as a democratically elected leader than he had been as a dictator, and unrest returned to the country. With a hint of civil war in the wind and the loss of support among the military, Var-

gas committed suicide in 1954. Historians have not yet decided what to make of Vargas, who is still a controversial figure in Brazil. The widest street in Rio is named in his honor.

Visionary Scheme

The presidency of Juscelino Kubitschek dealt Rio what might have seemed a heavy blow. He built Brasília, mobilizing the nation to transform a dusty plateau some 600 miles northwest of Rio into a working capital. Moving the government to the interior had been under half-hearted study for decades, but it was Kubitschek who helped make the world's most ambitious city-planning scheme a reality in just four years. In 1960 Brasília officially became the national capital, stripping Rio of almost two centuries of political power.

But surprisingly the city failed to wither away. Although most of the diplomats and federal officials eventually, reluctantly, accepted their transfers from beachfront to boondocks, miraculously their desks were filled by new legions of bureaucrats. Having lost the political crown to Brasília and the title of biggest and richest city to São Paulo, Rio still managed to prosper. The population kept growing – alarmingly.

For country folk migrating to the shores of Guanabara Bay – as for all the tourists – Rio needs no special credentials. Being one of the world's most cheerful and beautiful cities is quite enough. Rio faces no challenge for the heart of the Brazilian people.

What to See

The beauties of Rio are legend, though you'd hardly know it on the way in from the international airport – so don't be discouraged by first impressions of the Northern Zone's heavy industry.

Central Rio is a busy mixture of historic buildings over-shadowed by high-rise office blocks. The district is graced with sweeping gardens and the man-made beaches fronting Guanabara Bay. Tunnels through Rio's several hills link the center with the alluring Southern Zone (*Zona Sul*). This is the oceanfront area where the tourists and Rio's 'beautiful people' spend most of their time.

Sightseeing can be an ordeal under the tropical sun, so it's wisest not to wander aimlessly afoot. Decide where you want to go, then take a taxi or bus. Taxis are plentiful and economical, and for in-town travel they are the most convenient form of transport. For out-of-town trips, you can hire a car and drive yourself; and bus excursions go to many of the places described in this book.

Rio's bus service is good and cheap, but the complicated routes take some figuring out and many of the bus stops are unmarked.

Tourists climb Corcovado for a close-up of the Redeemer statue.

However, passengers and drivers always know which buses stop where – so ask for help.

Line One of the Metrô (underground, subway) goes all the way from the northern suburb of Tijuca to Botafogo, the south-zone district where Rio's elegant yacht club is located.

21

The ferryboats from Praça XV de Novembro offer very cheap sightseeing. Or you can view the bay from a luxury tour boat.

With so much to see and do, don't try to cover it all too fast. When the going gets hot, it's time to follow Carioca custom and head for the beach.

The glitter of Rio, crammed between the mountains and the sea.

Rio Panorama

Pão de Açúcar (Sugar Loaf) is such a well-known landmark that some visitors are surprised to find it's not as tall as, say, the Matterhorn or Mount Fuji. No one ever claimed it was any more than a dramatic rock standing guard over the entrance to Guanabara Bay. From its summit, 1,293 feet above sea level, you can read Rio like a map.

The only way to reach the top of Sugar Loaf is aboard a cable car which makes the journey in two stages. The trip begins at the Estação do Teleférico near Praia Vermelha (Red Beach). All the buses marked 'Urca' pass within a couple of blocks of the station. The first stage of the aerial itinerary takes you to the top of Morro da Urca, somewhat more than half as high as Sugar Loaf. At this way station, which also has

good panoramas over Rio, there's a big restaurant, as well as shops and a curious little museum of mechanized marionettes. The next car leaves for the Sugar Loaf summit, where you get an airline pilot's view of Rio and Guanabara Bay. In fact, you're high above the runway of Santos Dumont airport. There are several *mirantes* (observation points) overlooking Rio, but none more dramatic than this one – especially at sunset when the lights of the Marvelous City flicker on.

The overall travel time on the cable cars is only five or six minutes, with departures at least every 20 minutes and much more frequently during busy periods. Delays rarely occur, but if there's a sudden storm, safety-conscious officials may temporarily suspend traffic, stranding passengers at all levels (but not in mid-air). A more likely problem: if there's a cloud within 10 miles of Rio, it tends to sidle up to Sugar Loaf and spoil the view. Scrutinize the sky carefully before embarking on your cable-car adventure, lest you end up contemplating a wall of mist and drizzle.

At 2,326 feet, **Corcovado**, meaning Humpbacked Mountain, is nearly twice as high as Sugar

Loaf and no less symbolic. The statue of **Cristo Redentor** (Christ the Redeemer), with arms outstretched over the bay, was inaugurated as a national monument in 1931. The reinforced-concrete statue, designed by the French sculptor Paul Landowski, is 98 feet tall; a small chapel is built into its base A number of local, state and federal bureaus share responsibility for the site, so maintenance problems are chronic.

You can take a sightseeing tour of Rio that includes Corcovado. The buses stop halfway up the mountain and transfer passengers to smaller vehicles for the circuitous drive to the parking area, from which it's still a vigorous hike up to the base of the statue. Or you can take a taxi, or drive yourself. But the most enjoyable way to get to Corcovado is aboard the funicular which begins its ascent in Cosme Velho. All buses marked 'Cosme Velho' stop within a few steps of the funicular terminal (Estrada de Ferro Corcovado, 513 Rua Cosme Velho). A Swiss cable railway replaces a line opened by Emperor Pedro II in 1884. The trip takes about 20 minutes and passes through full-fledged jungle with brilliant flowering trees.

The view from the top of Corcovado is sensationally comprehensive – from the bay to the city center to the sea. Conversely the statue, which is well lighted at night, may be seen from almost any place in Rio – a symbol more ubiquitous than the Empire State Building or the Eiffel Tower.

If clouds are clinging to Corcovado, you may be able to sneak in under the cloud ceiling at another belvedere in the same area, the **Mirante Dona Marta** (1,191 feet). Luxuriant tropical plants surround the modern observation platforms, from which you have an excellent perspective on the spacious Lagoa Rodrigo de Freitas, a lagoon separated from the ocean by the communities of Ipanema and Leblon.

Corcovado and Dona Marta are within the **Parque Nacional da Tijuca** (Tijuca National Park), a precious wilderness inside Rio's city limits. Another belvedere in the same park is called Vista Chinesa (Chinese View), the lookout point being occupied by a pagoda-like structure. This is not quite the flight of fancy it may seem. In the early 19th century Chinese immigrants established a tea plantation on this site. (See p. 46.)

Historic Rio

Although remnants of colonial architecture can be seen in many parts of Rio, the greatest concentration of historic monuments centers on **Praça XV de Novembro** (November 15 Square). This was the city's main square long before it received its present name, commemorating the day in 1889 when the Brazilian republic was proclaimed. Though Praça XV suffers merciless motor traffic on two sides, it could have been worse. Over a century ago, it was the proposed site of the mouth of a projected tunnel to Niterói across the bay. But the big bore was abandoned. The engineers went back to their drawing boards, and in 1974 a bridge was

Commuters line up for the 'big ear' public telephones in front of the ferry station at Praça XV – the throbbing heart of Rio's historic district.

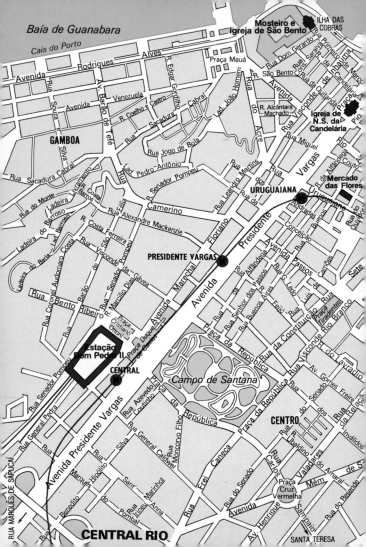

dedicated instead – but far north of Praça XV.

With the ferry station just across the road (it's safer to use the graceful pedestrian bridge), Praça XV is always a busy place. In addition to the customary popcorn vendors, lottery ticket salesmen and itinerant musicians, crowds of artists show up every Friday and Saturday to sell their works. Among the square's monuments are an equestrian statue of the King João VI (a gift from Portugal in 1965) near the ferry terminal and an 18th-century fountain by the sculptor known as Mestre Valentim.

With your back to the bay, the elegant three-story colonial building on your left is the **Palácio dos Vice-Reis,** the former residence of the Portuguese viceroys, completed in 1743. As the city's fortunes rose, the building was pressed into service as the royal (later imperial) palace. At the beginning of the 20th century it was relegated to the post-office department – then in 1985 the fully renovated palace was reinaugurated as a cultural center.

Across Rua 1° de Março from the square there are two 18th-century churches separated only by a narrow passageway. The one on the left, with a tall corner bell tower, is the **Igreja de Nossa Senhora do Carmo** (Carmelite Church), the former cathedral. In this Portuguese baroque church, the emperor of Brazil was crowned. A plaque in the corridor of the sacristy covers an urn which is said to have contained the ashes of Cabral, the Portuguese explorer who discovered Brazil. In 1976, this cathedral lost its title to the newly built Metropolitan Cathedral above Avenida República do Chile.

The fine baroque interior of the former cathedral is relatively modest compared with the **Igreja de Nossa Senhora do Monte do Carmo** (Church of Our Lady of Mount Carmel), right next door. Notice the exuberant decorations on the walls, the rich altar and the marble works of Mestre Valentim, the creator of the Praça XV fountain. At the far end of the walkway between the two churches, over a gate, stands one of the few public oratories remaining in Rio. An electric light has replaced the original oil lamp illuminating the image in this little shrine.

Another architectural feature is located on the north side of Praça XV: the **Arco do Teles,** an archway cutting through a long, low building to the next street. The passageway is unusual for its width and general stateliness.

The charming 18th-century **Igreja de Nossa Senhora da Lapa dos Mercadores** (Lapa Merchants' Church) is hidden around the corner at 35 Rua do Ouvidor. An unexpected item on display is a used artillery shell dated 1893. During a naval rebellion, this was accidentally fired at the tower of the church, dislodging a large marble statue of the Virgin Mary. The delicate statue fell several floors to earth, miraculously breaking nothing more than the tips of two of its fingers.

Rua do Ouvidor, which runs from the port to Avenida Rio Branco and beyond, has been a thriving pedestrian street since 1829. It was one of the first three streets in Rio to be lit by gas (1854). In those days newspaper offices, as well as fashionable foreign-owned shops and restaurants, were located here. Rua do Ouvidor has had at least a dozen different names over the years, but none the authorities imposed ever caught the public imagination. 'Ouvidor', which means 'overseer', is what people always called it, after a noted official whose house was here; and in the end the people won the battle of the names. The street is very lively any working day, which is why it is thronged with blind lottery-ticket sellers enjoying immunity from Rio drivers.

It is very difficult to cross Avenida Presidente Vargas, a thoroughfare 180 feet wide. Only the very alert are competent to navigate from one side to the other across so many lanes of unpredictable traffic. President Getúlio Vargas immodestly attended the military parade in 1944 at which the avenue was named after himself.

Avenida Vargas starts at Praça Pio X (Pius X Square), containing the cathedral-sized **Igreja de Nossa Senhora da Candelária.** Construction of this sumptuous church with Italianate features went on from about 1775 to 1810. The interior is entirely decorated with marble of remarkably varied colors: black, white, gray, yellow, green, red. Thanks to the Avenida Vargas project, which demolished many nearby buildings (including three other churches), the Candelária church now stands in distinguished isolation at a dramatic crossroads.

Although you can't miss the Candelária church, you won't be **29**

able to find your way to the **Igreja e Mosteiro de São Bento** (St Bento Church and Monastery) without knowing a secret. The trick is to walk down Rua Dom Gerardo, slip into an unmarked modern building at number 40, and take the elevator to the top floor. The roof of the building leads to the grounds of the church and monastery. (You can also do it the harder way, via the gate at number 68 Rua Dom Gerardo and a long walk uphill.)

São Bento provides a cool, quiet escape from the city's bustle. The church, part of a Benedictine monastery, was begun in 1633. Its simple but strong façade has twin towers capped with pyramids; large arched doorways with wrought-iron gates lead to 17th-century portals of finely carved wood. Inside, the florid decor reaches up to a painted, vaulted ceiling from which hang two heavy chandeliers.

To visit the monastery adjoining the church, advance permission is required; only men are admitted, except when special processions are held.

Rio's church interiors are conducive to divine contemplation.

Central Rio

In the city's main street, **Avenida Rio Branco**, you will find some impressive banks, airline offices and neoclassic public buildings. At the start of the 20th century, the layout seemed quite far-sighted: a perfectly straight road, over a mile long, with a row of brazilwood trees down the middle. Thirty-two pavers were sent over from Lisbon to build Portuguese-style mosaic sidewalks. But the brazilwood trees and trolley-car tracks ultimately gave way to the internal-combustion engine; and today, even though traffic is one-way, the congestion can cause heights of frustration.

Originally named Avenida Central, the street was retitled in 1912 in honor of the Baron of Rio Branco, the unusually able foreign minister, who had just died.

Sometime during your stay in Rio, you'll probably have business to transact in Avenida Rio Branco – at an airline office, a travel agency, shop, bank or currency exchange office. Take advantage of the trip and look over the soberly dressed businessmen bouncing from big deal to coffee break, the messenger boys and hawkers zigzagging through the viscous crowds, and the provincials gawking at all the activity. You can even find restaurant tables for relaxed people-watching.

At the corner of Rio Branco and Rua do Ouvidor look for the small statue called *Monumento ao Pequeno Jornaleiro*. Erected in 1931 by the newspaper *A Noite*, now extinct, it is said to be the only monument anywhere honoring the lads who peddle newspapers on the streets.

One place you wouldn't have thought about for your shopping is **Rua da Alfândega** (Customshouse Street), which parallels Avenida Vargas almost from the port to Praça da República. This long pedestrian street is where Cariocas go for bargains in clothing, household appliances and knick-knacks. The variety of objects for sale is fascinating. Because so many of the open-fronted stores are owned by merchants of Arab or Jewish descent, the western end of the street is known colloquially as the Saara (Sahara). A notice proudly proclaims 'In Saara, you are a very important person' and the area's selling techniques back it up, with pop music and radio-station publicity blaring from loudspeakers strung across the street. **31**

Sign Here, Please

It sounds like something out of *Alice in Wonderland* or *Catch-22*, but Brazil really has a Secretary of Debureaucratization.

You can thank the ministry for abolishing eight of the 25 snoopy questions every tourist must answer on arrival at a Brazilian hotel. The hotel industry had long complained that most visitors either laughed or cried when confronted with the long official questionnaire.

But in spite of these triumphs of debureaucratization, it will be some time before Brazil levels its red-tape jungle. A teenager applying for a part-time job still has to obtain nine different documents and six identification pictures. And the thump of rubber stamps echoes through the land.

If you've wandered as far as the Sahara, go another few steps into the oasis of **Praça da República** (Republic Square). This century-old public park, also known as Campo de Santana, is large enough and fertile enough to repel the big-city heat and noise that surround it. Vast fichu trees with roots above and below the ground provide the shade. Ducks and swans inhabit the ponds, and agouti (rodents halfway between squirrels and guinea pigs) romp on the lawns.

From here, and from almost anywhere on the north side of Rio, you can see the biggest clock in town, occupying six floors of the tower above the **Estação Dom Pedro II** (Dom Pedro II Railway Station). There are clock faces on all four sides of the tower, all electronically synchronized. The minute hands alone are almost 25 feet long. Down at street level, 130,000 commuters arrive and depart on suburban trains every day. There's a Metrô station here, too.

Two-thirds of the way from the railway station to Praça XV de Novembro, at Praça Olavo Bilac, is the Rio flower market *(Mercado das Flores)*. All the shops here sell plants or fresh flowers – not only roses and carnations, but exotic bird-of-paradise flowers, another reminder that you're in the tropics. Nearby, furtive men with small carbon-papered order books lurk in wait for customers of the numbers racket. The *jogo do bicho* (animal game), though officially illegal, seems an indispensable part of Rio life. Each of 25 animals, from *avestruz* (ostrich) to *vaca* (cow), represents four numbers. Any Carioca who has dreamed of, say, a butterfly (*borboleta*) rushes to the nearest numbers agent to bet on 13 through 16. Results come in twice a day, so the suspense only has to be endured for a couple of hours.

For a bit of history in a teacup, stroll down nearby Rua Gonçalves Dias. The Confeitaria Colombo, Rio's most fashionable tearoom since the turn of the century, stops the clock with its elegant decor. Giant Belgian mirrors on all the walls double the effect of the Louis XV-style furnishings. At certain times of day, the place is filled with matrons out of the same mold as the tea: pastry and gossip enthusiasts of 1912. At other times, businessmen or trendy show-business figures dominate; tea is by no means the only brew consumed on these relaxed premises.

Rua Gonçalves Dias runs into Largo da Carioca, a small park which was once a lagoon. The Metrô construction has resulted in a rather austere landscape, but nothing has changed on the promontory above, occupied by two colonial-era churches.

The **Igreja e Convento de Santo Antônio** (St Anthony's Church and Convent), on the left, was founded at the beginning of the 17th century. St Anthony is an exceedingly popular saint in Rio, as in his native Lisbon, so the church is often packed – especially every Tuesday and on certain holidays. An elevator inside the hill saves steps for some of the visitors. The convent, which at one time housed more than a hundred Franciscan friars, has a spacious cloister and several interesting chapels.

The church next door to St Anthony's has the awesome title of **Igreja da Venerável Ordem Terceira de São Francisco da Penitência** (Church of the Venerable Third Order of St Francis of the Penitence). The beautiful 18th-century interior is lavishly decorated – a veritable treasure-house of distinguished baroque workmanship in wood, gilt and marble. As you enter the church, notice the saintly statues on each side – both with moustaches!

Critics of architecture vehemently disagree about the new **Catedral Metropolitana**, also called Catedral Nova, rising like a volcano on the horizon southwest of the convent complex. The design of the reinforced-concrete and glass structure has been described as a truncated cone or an Etruscan pyramid. The cornerstone was laid in 1964. The nave, which is longer than a football field, can accommodate 20,000 standing worshippers. Gigantic stained-glass windows of bold modern design, one for each quadrant, flood the interior with sunlight. A plaque at the main entrance commemorates the day Pope John Paul II preached at the cathedral: July 2, 1980.

In contrast to the circular floor-plan of the cathedral, the cubic **Petrobrás** building just across the street is all right angles. With gaping chunks seemingly cut out of the façade to make landscaped balconies, it resembles a three-dimensional crossword puzzle. Roberto Burle Marx designed the landscaping for Petrobrás, the Brazilian state-owned oil monopoly.

Engineers and architects designing a new plan for this dynamic part of Rio could take

inspiration from the work of their 18th-century predecessors, who created a utilitarian monument that's still standing, still beautiful and still working. **Arcos da Carioca** (The Carioca Aqueduct) – otherwise called *Os Arcos* (The Arches) – looks as if the Romans got to Rio first, but it was actually put into operation in 1750.

A cooling ice-cream cone; and the striking conical Cathedral.

The double-deck archway started a new life in 1896, when the city's water supply was diverted to more modern channels. The monument then became a viaduct for a tram line linking central Rio with the hills of Santa Teresa. Astoundingly, the trams – affectionately called *bondinhos* – still rattle across the narrow bridge.

There are faster ways to reach the pleasant district of Santa Teresa, but the *bondinho*, Rio's

last surviving tram line, is more fun. The conductor moves along the running board collecting fares en route; and youngsters leap on and off the moving tram to avoid paying. The tracks twist and turn sharply on the steep hillsides. It's almost as exciting as a San Francisco cable car.

Culture and Movieland

Back to Avenida Rio Branco, the city's main street, which abandons commerce for culture in its southernmost few blocks.

The **Teatro Municipal**, an opera house which opened in 1909, looks solid and solemn enough for its role. From its stage Nijinsky, Pavlova, Caruso and Toscanini brought culture to the Cariocas. A side entrance leads to a meticulously restored gala restaurant which serves lunches and after-opera suppers.

Two more neoclassical buildings from the same era complete the ensemble here. Across Avenida Rio Branco is the **Museu Nacional de Belas Artes** (National Fine Arts Museum); the architect was inspired by the Louvre in Paris. For details of the exhibits, see p. 51. Opposite, the **Palácio Pedro Ernesto** was inaugurated in 1923 as the home of the state assembly. It now belongs to the city council. Taxpayers from any city in the world will be impressed by the majestic decorations inside and out.

Here begins the pleasantly tiled and gardened plaza officially called Praça Floriano. Around this square the best movie theaters of Rio sprang up in the 1930s and 40s, hence the popular name for the area, **Cinelândia.** Cariocas don't go to the movies as often as they used to, and the cinemas of the Zona Sul offer strong competition; but Cinelândia remains a lively part of town. Artists and artisans often set up stands here to sell their works, and street musicians play to the crowds. Even if nothing's doing, you can take a seat at an outdoor café and wait for the excitement.

A final Victorian palace of note: the **Biblioteca Nacional** (National Library), on the far side of Avenida Rio Branco. With about three million items, the collection is considered the most important in South America. Take a look at the vast reading room just off the lobby. It must be the quietest place in Rio.

Antique tram on an 18th-century viaduct in the modern city center.

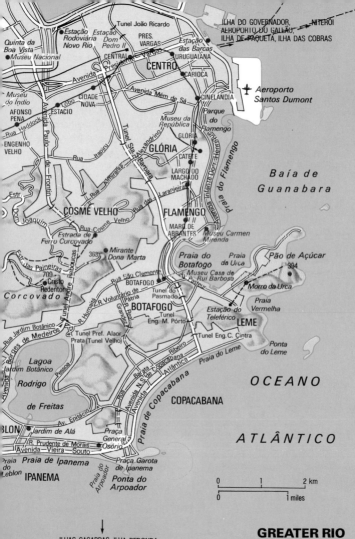

GREATER RIO

Beaches

Copacabana and Ipanema, Rio's two most renowned beaches, cover more than four miles of glamorous sandy coast. But Rio has many more beaches to choose from – intimate or endless, busy or deserted, with or without waves – all open to the public without restriction or charge.

For the price of a lemonade, you can ride a bus that hugs the coast for 20 miles or more, travel in your swimsuit if you want, and ring the bell when you see the beach of your dreams. Here's a rundown, starting within walking distance of the center of town, continuing along the harbor, then past Sugar Loaf to the Zona Sul beaches facing the Atlantic.

Stacks of colorful beach loungers await Copacabana sunbathers.

Flamengo. The beach closest to the business district, Flamengo is the first to get crowded, even though there's a vast stretch of bright sand. This man-made beach forms part of the venturesome Flamengo Park project, which pushed Rio's front garden out into the harbor. There are no waves to worry about, but harbor waters are murky; swimmers prefer the unpolluted ocean beaches.

Botafogo. Another man-made harborside beach of brilliant white sand. Sharing the cove here are the big and small pleasure boats of the Rio Yacht Club.

Urca. Barely 100 yards long, this beach is squeezed in under Sugar Loaf, with striking views of the Rio skyline.

Vertmelha. On the south side of Sugar Loaf, 'Red Beach' has a view of almost uninterrupted hills and islands. Because it's small and close to town, this beach of coarse dark sand tends to fill up with sunbathers.

Leme. Now we're on the open Atlantic, facing south and taking the rollers. Before the Túnel Novo opened in 1904, it was an adventure to reach this point. Now it's only the beginning of the busy stretch of Zona Sul's most popular beaches. Actually,

Leme is the name of the first kilometer (reading from east to west) of Copacabana Beach. In earlier times a lifeguard station was established every kilometer, and Leme was 'Posto 1'.

Copacabana, which runs all the way to Posto 6, where small fishing boats are beached, is more beautiful today than when it first caught the world's imagination. A massive and messy reclamation project extended the beach far out to sea and widened the oceanside avenue and pedestrian areas. Almost all buses have been diverted from Avenida Atlântica, and the beachside walkway – paved with black and white stones in the undulating Portuguese style – is wide enough for all the strollers, joggers and sightseers. A cycle route runs alongside. On the landward side of the avenue, sidewalk cafés at crucial intervals supply Cariocas with that essential *chopinho* (ice-cold draft beer).

In the early 1920s Avenida Atlântica, at that time unpaved, was lined with the private houses of adventurous Cariocas. Then came the first hotel, the Copacabana Palace, which was grand enough to entertain the likes of Roosevelt and de Gaulle, Eva Perón and Lana Turner, Chiang

Kai-shek and Emperor Hirohito – which is how the beach achieved worldwide fame. Visiting kings still turn up at the Copa Palace now and then, but five-star sky-scraper hotels along the beach have long since broken its monopoly on luxury and comfort. Except for one private house still holding out against the astronomical offers of real-estate speculators, the avenue is now devoted to expensive high-rise apartment houses and hotels. Many of these buildings have restaurants on the ground floor, usually with open fronts facing the ocean and outdoor tables under sun umbrellas. But Avenida Atlântic a is almost devoid of shops, apart from the little street stalls selling bikinis, leather goods and Brazilian souvenirs. The main shopping street is one block inland, Avenida Nossa Senhora de Copacabana, or Copacabana Avenue.

The peninsula separating Copacabana from **Ipanema** beach ends in a rocky outcrop called Ponta do Arpoador. On the east side of it, a small beach aptly named Praia do Diabo (Devil's Beach) has permanent 'danger' signs posted. The very strong tide here still inspires some surfers, but the ideal place for surfing is just the other side of this narrow neck of land, at **Arpoador** beach.

A hilly municipal park named **Praça Garota de Ipanema** (Girl from Ipanema Plaza) honors the song, and the girls, responsible for the area's fame. These girls, in their ingeniously designed minimal swimsuits, are the most eye-opening attraction. But if you can look up from the fine-sand beach, notice the coconut

Sunbathers buying ice-cold mate, the Gaucho drink. Enthusiasm for Rio's miles of beaches is shared by tourists and Cariocas alike.

palms and, behind them, the elegant apartment houses enhanced by landscaping and sculpture. For reasons such as these, Ipanema is considered more fashionable than Copacabana – and the most fashionable spot of all, at last report, is the stretch of beach in front of Rua Vinícius de Mor-

rais. Brazil's pioneer devotees of toplessness first unveiled their enthusiasms here, bringing out hordes of gawkers. Inland, along the streets of Ipanema are found the most chic boutiques in all of Rio. Fashion of all sorts is the big talking point. Ipanema also has many of Rio's favorite bars and **43** restaurants, full of atmosphere and loyal perennial clients.

Leblon. This relaxed beach, the extension of Ipanema, is divided from its bigger and more famous sister by a canal flanked by gardens with the evocative name of **Jardim de Alá** (Garden of Allah). The waterway joins the sea with Rio's lagoon, **Lagoa Rodrigo de Freitas**. Even if Rio had no ocean, no bay, no Sugar Loaf, the skyline as seen from the lagoon would still qualify it as a thoroughly enticing city. Surrounded by parks and urban developments, the lagoon is large enough for motorboat races, calm enough for pedal boats. Along its shore are clubs, sports grounds and the Tivoli amusement park.

After Leblon the coast road, called Avenida Niemeyer, twists along the rugged side of Pedra Dois Irmãos (Two Brothers Rock). Part of the hillside, which rises to an altitude of 1,500 feet, is occupied by a *favela*. Below is **Vidigal** beach, a pretty 600-yard-long stretch of sand.

São Conrado, a beach almost a mile long, begins opposite the giant cylindrical Hotel National. Strong tides here suggest that bathers swim with caution. Sunbathers have the added diversion of watching hang-gliders taking their time about descending 1,700 feet from the launching site on Pedra Bonita hill. Eventually they alight on the west end of São Conrado beach.

Some elaborate engineering, including double-deck tunnels and viaducts, carries the westward highway along and through the precipitous hillsides to the up-and-coming resort of **Barra da Tijuca**. Backed by lagoons, this is Rio's longest beach by far:

11 miles of sand that seem to stretch to infinity. Barra is noted for its seafood restaurants. But on the big beach, beware of the dangerous ocean currents.

Inland from Barra is the Riocentro convention center. If you are in Rio in November, don't miss the giant charity fair (*Feira da Providência*) here. Also watch for the Brazilian Formula One Grand Prix, held annually at the Autódromo, next to Riocentro.

A great rock marks the end of the classic beach of Barra. Beyond that is **Recreio dos Bandeirantes**, a beach over a mile long, with rough seas. Strong surf also limits the possibilities at the next beach, called **Prainha** (Little Beach), set beneath pretty green hills. **Grumari**, a fishing village, has a small beach with red-tinted sand.

Barra de Guaratiba, the first of the beaches on the splendid **Bay of Sepetiba**, is a fetching spot surrounded by trees. All the bay beaches have delightfully calm seas. Beyond, the Zona Sul beach **Sepetiba** has the same tranquil waters, plus the convenience of bars and restaurants nearby. If medicinal mud sounds inviting, the strand at Sepetiba has just what the doctor ordered.

Green Rio

Rio de Janeiro is a city of astonishingly diverse parks, ranging from primeval forest to carefully cultivated modern gardens. Here are some of the biggest and best:

Jardim Botânico (Botanical Garden). It would be a pity not to visit this delightfully fragrant enclave on Rua Jardim Botânico, the busy avenue that connects the Leblon and Botafogo districts. Dom João VI, then prince regent, founded the garden in 1808 – alongside the royal gunpowder factory. In 1809 the *Palma Mater*, the mother of all the royal palm trees in Brazil, was planted here; the seeds had been imported – stolen, actually – from the Indian Ocean island now called Mauritius. The palmiest of all palms grew to be 127 feet high and lived to the age of 164, when it was felled by a lightning bolt. Avenues of descendant royal palms still tower over everything else in this garden and forest.

Among other highlights are six lakes, including a pond where enormous lilies float like platters with upturned edges; the orchid nursery; and a special hothouse for insectivorous plants. As luck would have it, the best time to see **45** flowers in bloom is outside the main tourist season. But at any time of year there's plenty to see.

Parque da Cidade (City Park). Beyond the botanical garden in Gávea, just before the Dois Irmãos tunnel, is the entrance to this quiet park. Formerly the estate of the Marques of São Vicente, it was opened to the public in 1941. Aside from an interesting range of trees, the estate has expanses of lawn and also its own little river and lake. The former manor house has become the Museu da Cidade (City Historical Museum), with fine old furniture, historic banners and weapons, and prints and paintings showing Rio's role in Brazil's past.

Parque Nacional da Tijuca (Tijuca National Park). Here, within the confines of a great metropolis, is all the jungle you'll ever want to see – and some breezy heights for relief from the heat. Excursion companies run half-day bus tours of the park and its best-known peak, Corcovado (see p. 23). Or you can ask a taxi driver to show you the highlights of this enormous forest (make sure you fix a price before you leave).

In the early colonial development of Rio, the thick forests of the Tijuca mountainsides were felled for lumber and firewood. The land was then used for orchards and coffee plantations. A reforestation program was undertaken in the middle of the 19th century, when Cariocas began to realize that the wilderness of Tijuca was well worth saving.

In addition to the park's lookout points (see p. 24), watch for these attractions:

Cascatinha de Taunay, a waterfall, is named after the 19th-century French artist Nicolas Antoine Taunay, who lived nearby. On a hot day the gently tumbling waters of this cascade are a thoroughly refreshing sight!

Capela Mayrink was the private chapel of the Mayrink family, who lived in the park in the 19th century. This small, brightly colored building, renovated in 1944, contains much-admired religious paintings.

The park also has more waterfalls, caves, lookouts – including **Mesa do Imperador** (The Emperor's Table), a beauty spot where the imperial family used to enjoy the view and a picnic – and three restaurants.

Parque do Flamengo. This challenging project gave Rio de Janeiro a facelift of which any

Visitors admiring the Botanical Garden's giant water lilies, with an umbrella to ward off the sun.

city could be justifiably proud. In a colossal landfill program, completed in 1960, nearly 300 acres were reclaimed from the harbor. Brazil's master landscape architect, Roberto Burle Marx, transformed the new terrain into an admirable green belt between the sea and the city, with room enough for a superhighway, monuments, museums and all manner of leisure facilities.

47

The park, so conveniently located on the edge of the business district, tends to fill up on weekends, starting with its beach, over half a mile long. The most popular sport on the playing fields behind the beach is soccer; and informal matches, often with the players barefoot, go on virtually 24 hours a day.

Palms soothe and beautify Rio's fashionable Flamengo district.

On Sundays traffic is barred from the highway through the park, permitting roller skaters, cyclists and joggers to fan out over the wide-open asphalt.

As in many parts of Rio, kites are often launched here – though they face tough competition from powered model airplanes.

One way to get the feel of Flamengo Park is to take the *trenzinho* (little train), a tractor-drawn sightseeing vehicle which covers

most of the grounds in 25 minutes. Children enjoy it most, but adults are fully welcome aboard.

Overlooking the park from a bluff that was once right alongside the harbor is a church so appealing you may want to take the funicular up for a look. The simple, harmonious lines of the **Igreja de Nossa Senhora da Glória do Outeiro** (Gloria Church on the Hill) date from 1714. During the 19th century the royal family often came here for baptisms, non-ceremonial private devotions and the like. Inside, the church's walls are decorated with classic Portuguese *azulejos* (blue-and-white decorative tiles).

After a lookout over the harbor, take the zig-zag stepped path down past the remains of candles and other traces of macumba on the stone benches and rock face.

This section of the city is named Glória, so the yacht basin in Flamengo Park is called the Marina da Glória. Unlike the Rio Yacht Club in Botafogo, with its millionaire membership, the Marina da Glória is open to anyone.

Flamengo Park also contains three museums. Reading from north to south, the first is the **Museu de Arte Moderna** (Modern Art Museum), often referred to as MAM. A daring architectural scheme of the 1950s, the building stands on stilts and is surrounded by richly integrated gardens. In 1978 it suffered a catastrophic fire which spared the structure but devoured the museum's paintings. The collection had included works by Dali, Ernst, Matisse, Miró, Picasso and Pollock, as well as Brazilian artists. It will be years before the MAM can begin to recover, if ever. In the meantime, temporary exhibits are planned.

Museu do Monumento aos Mortos da Segunda Guerra (Museum of the Monument to the Dead of World War II). This museum is part of a monumental ensemble topped by slim twin pillars that appear to form the Roman numeral II. On display are weapons, gas masks, helmets and captured battle flags recalling the Brazilian contribution to the campaign against the German army in Italy.

Museu Carmen Miranda. In a modern circular building tucked away in the trees of Flamengo Park, fans of the late 'Brazilian Bombshell' can view more than 1,500 items of nostalgia – jewelry, photos and costumes, including those incredible hats.

Outstanding Museums

Museu Nacional. One of the oldest scientific institutions in Latin America, Brazil's National Museum was established in 1818 by King João VI. The three-story palace it now occupies was the residence of the royal family for 81 years. Specializing in anthropology and the natural sciences, the National Museum is the sort of place delegations of school children visit, in order to gape at dinosaur skeletons, mummies, stuffed birds and Brazilian Indian artifacts, ranging from ceremonial adornments to curare darts. The star exhibit, however, is a meteorite that fell to earth in the state of Bahia in 1888, weighing more than five tons. Prudently, the museum officials decided to leave it on the ground floor.

Since it is on the northern side of Rio, the National Museum is out of the way for most tourists; but it makes a handy 'package tour' with the neighboring zoo (see p. 54). Moreover, the museum grounds, called the Quinta da Boa Vista, are big enough to support a *trenzinho* for sightseeing. The Quinta's lake accommodates both pedal boats and swimmers.

Museu da República. (The Museum of the Republic – reopened after structural repairs). This regal palace served as the official residence of the presidents of Brazil from 1896 to 1954 – when Getúlio Vargas killed himself in his third-floor bedroom. Everything in this mid-19th-century residence – floors, ceilings, walls, mirrors, chandeliers, furniture – is sensationally well done, an opulent prize worth preserving. The Second Empire decorations and furnishings are so stunning that the exhibits recounting the history of the republic and its presidents may seem something of an anticlimax.

The building that houses the museum – called the Palácio do Catete – has had a checkered history. Completed in 1866 for the Baron of Nova Friburgo, it was converted into a hotel in 1890. Bankruptcy propelled it into the hands of the government. The palace's gardens, with its rows of royal palms, extend right to the boundary of Flamengo Park.

Museu Histórico Nacional. The history of the National Historical Museum's premises is nearly as interesting as its contents. Established in 1922, the museum took over one of the old-

Cariocas dress casually, even for an outing to the stately National Museum. The grounds of this former royal palace lead to the zoo.

est buildings in Rio de Janeiro, the 16th-century Fortaleza de São Tiago (St James Fortress); its cellars were once used as dungeons for slaves. Later, the building served as a military prison, an arsenal and the headquarters of the Royal Military Academy.

The public entrance to the museum's huge irregularly shaped compound faces the main waterfront highway, near Praça XV de Novembro. You don't have to be well versed in Brazilian history to appreciate the displays of ceremonial swords and helmets, thrones and palatial furnishings. One room is devoted to exhibits on slavery, such as torture instruments and manacles. In the patio, 19th-century gala coaches look as if they are ready to leave for a coronation at any moment.

Museu Nacional de Belas Artes. Occupying a ponderous palace on the busy Avenida Rio Branco, the National Fine Arts Museum conscientiously follows 51

Museum Finder

To avoid disappointment, check on opening hours before you go.

São Cristóvão

Museu Nacional, Quinta da Boa Vista. Tuesday–Sunday 10 am–4.30 pm, tel. 264-8262

Jardim Zoológico, Quinta da Boa Vista. Tuesday–Sunday 9 am–4.30 pm, tel. 254-2024

Santa Teresa

Museu Chácara do Céu, Rua Murtinho Nobre, 93. Tuesday–Saturday 2–5 pm, Sunday 1–5 pm, tel. 232-1386.

Center

Museu Histórico Nacional, Praça Mal. Âncora, s/no. Tuesday–Friday 10 am–5.30 pm, Saturday and Sunday 2.30–5.30 pm, tel. 220 5450.

Museu Naval e Oceanográfico, Rua Dom Manuel, 15. Daily 12–4.30 pm, tel. 221-7626.

Museu da Imagem e do Som, Praça Rui Barbosa, 1. Monday–Friday 1–6 pm, tel. 262-0309.

Museu Nacional de Belas Artes, Avenida Rio Branco, 199. Tuesday–Friday 10.00–6 pm, Saturday and Sunday 3–6 pm, tel. 240-0160.

Flamengo

Museu de Arte Moderna, Avenida Infante Dom Henrique, 85. Parque do Flamengo. Tuesday–Saturday 12–7 pm (till 10 pm on Thursday), Sunday 2–7 pm, tel. 210-2188. (Hours are changeable, so check before you visit).

Museu do Monumento aos Mortos da Segunda Guerra Mundial, Avenida Infante Dom Henrique, 75. Daily 10 am–5 pm, tel. 240-1283

Museu Carmen Miranda, Parque do Flamengo, Avenida Rui Barbosa, 560. Tuesday–Friday 11 am–5 pm, Saturday and Sunday 1–5 pm, tel. 551-2597.

Museu da República, Palácio do Catete, Rua do Catete, 153. Tuesday–Sunday 12–5pm, tel. 225 4302.

Botafogo

Museu Casa de Rui Barbosa, Rua São Clemente, 134. Tuesday–Friday 1–4 pm, admission every hour, tel. 286-1297 ext. 45

Museu do Índio, Rua das Palmeiras, 55. Tuesday–Friday 11.30 am–5 pm, Sunday 1–5 pm, tel. 286-2097.

the history of Brazilian painting from 18th-century academics to trendsetting modernists. Among those represented are Eliseu Visconti with his young nudes; José Almeida Junior, author of frank insights into rural life; and Cândido Portinari, whose view of life on a coffee plantation is moving and impressive. Another interesting painting is an informative seascape by 19th-century artist Nicolau Facchinetti. It shows that nothing has changed about Ilha Fiscal in Guanabara Bay – except that in those days it really was an island (it's now attached to Rio's navy base). The museum also has works by Flemish, French, German and Italian artists. On the outer walls of the building, contemporary artists often hang their latest works in hopes of finding a buyer among the passers-by.

Museu Chácara do Céu. This is as lovable a little museum as you'll find anywhere, and the setting is idyllic. Chácara do Céu means 'Little House of Heaven'. The house in question, an airy modern structure, sits in a manicured garden on a Santa Teresa hilltop surveying just about all of Rio. The house and the artworks (about 360 pieces both ancient and modern) show the personali-ty of the collector, Raymundo Ottoni de Castro May – one of the founders of the Museum of Modern Art, who died in 1968. The highlights of the collection include a 7th-century Chinese running horse; an 18th-century Persian carpet; Indian religious paintings of the same era; paintings by Monet, Modigliani and Picasso; and 21 radiant Don Quixote drawings by Portinari.

Other Museums in Brief

Museu do Índio (Indian Museum). A bit off the beaten track in Botafogo, this unprepossessing museum tells you how to read Indian symbols meaning 'Keep Out' or 'Danger' – if you understand the explanatory notes in Portuguese. See the appealing ceramics in unusual colors, headdresses of all ranks, dolls and musical instruments, and a huge drum for long-distance calls.

Museu Casa de Rui Barbosa. Guides speaking English and French (a considerable novelty in Rio) take visitors through the old mansion of the erudite Brazilian statesman, lawyer and orator Rui Barbosa de Oliveira (1849–1923). Take a look at Rui's 37,000-book personal library or his four antique cars.

Fun and Games

Jardim Zoológico. 'Não Dê Alimento Aos Animais' means 'Do not feed the animals' – but even literate Brazilians blithely disregard the signs. Like many of the visitors, the animals seem seized by tropical languor except at the official feeding times. (Nobody told the hippopotamus it's dangerous to go swimming after a big lunch.) Along with the usual run of lions, camels, elephants and monkeys, Rio's zoo has some 1,600 birds – including extremely rare tropical species – and, on the ground, a notable variety of panthers. Adults pay a minimal admission charge, and to avoid having children lie about their age the authorities have devised this system: any child who can walk *under* a turnstile 3 feet 11 inches high is admitted free.

Maracanã. Is it a monument, a museum, or just a sports stadium? Nobody in Rio would ever call Maracanã 'just' a stadium. The biggest soccer stadium in the world – capacity between 170,000 and 200,000, depending on how tightly the standing spectators can be squeezed in – is a sight to see even when it's empty. Guided tours take visitors behind

Museu Naval e Oceanográfico. Near Praça XV de Novembro, the collection features real guns, torpedoes and bombs, and also model ships and submarines.

Museu da Imagem e do Som (Museum of Image and Sound). Serious students mine its archives of musical scores, records, photographs and books on Carioca music. There are also exhibitions about the cultural currents of Rio.

Both outside and inside the vast Maracanã stadium enthusiasm explodes in carnival atmosphere.

the scenes, from the press bar to the players' dressing rooms and baths. (Notice the oxygen taps for half-time rejuvenation.) On match days the tours end early to clear the facilities for the players.

Even if you're not a soccer fan, you'll be impressed by the size of the place. As the guides recite, 'If the 500,000 bags of cement used in the construction were piled high, they would exceed the altitude of the Empire State Building.' With all its complex facilities, Maracanã was rushed to completion in less than two years for the World Cup of 1950 (Brazil lost to Uruguay). Since then, much soccer history has been made in the arena.

Guanabara Bay

Rio's momentous **harbor** has an area of about 160 square miles – room enough for supertankers, warships, tramp steamers, ferryboats, yachts and dozens of islands and islets. To cross from Rio de Janeiro to Niterói, which is physically and psychologically akin to leaving Manhattan for Staten Island, you can take the cheapest ferryboat in town or a high-flying hydrofoil. Or you can ride a bus or drive a car across the bold new six-lane toll bridge which marches across the bay on heavy stilts. The **bridge**, opened in 1974, is 8½ miles long, with more than half the distance over water. Its apogee in the middle of the bay is high enough to let any ship pass.

There are numerous sights to see in and across the bay – but when all is said and done, the best views are looking back at the grandeur of Rio de Janeiro. You used to be able to cover the waterfront by taking a Bateau Mouche (waterbus tour) but these were discontinued in the late 1980s following a tragic accident. You can however still ride the venerable **ferryboats** that carry commuters between Praça XV de Novembro and the city of Niterói in about 20 minutes.

Even leaving the Estação das Barcas (Boat Station) is fascinating. To your right (starboard side) is the main runway of Rio's in-town airport, Santos Dumont; planes come and go right over the harbor at disconcertingly low altitudes. To your left (port side) the **Ilha das Cobras** (Snake Island) belongs to the navy; on the far side you can see Brazil's only aircraft carrier, paradoxically named after the landlocked state of Minas Gerais, at its mooring. A roadway connects Ilha das Cobras with a small government island called **Ilha Fiscal**. The green fortress with bizarre towers in Arabian Nights style was inaugurated in 1889. Emperor Pedro II, who meddled with the architect and builders over several years, must take some of the blame.

Some tourists become disoriented here. Beyond the bridge, to your left, is the inner harbor; to your right, you should know, is the open sea. For defensive pur-

The slow and fast ways to Niterói: eager commuters flock together on ferry prows.

The charming villas, luxuriant foliage and relaxed pace make Paquetá an ideal place to visit.

poses the entrance to the harbor, below Sugar Loaf, could hardly be excelled. A small low-lying island, now fortified to resemble a weird whale with gun turrets, straddles the narrow opening between two 16th-century forts.

The ferry commuters ignore these curiosities, as well as the dazzling view of the Rio skyline. They read their newspapers, doze off, or enjoy the breeze with their feet hanging over the unprotected front edge of the forward deck.

Deep in the bay, just over an hour's ferry ride from Rio, lies a lush green island of merciful tranquility. **Paquetá** enjoys a total lack of cars. The only motorized vehicles are a very few delivery vans and an ambulance. To get around the mostly unpaved roads of the island, residents and tourists rely on bicycles, horse-drawn carriages and a so-called bus – actually a tractor-powered 'train' on rubber tires – which does a circuit of Paquetá in less than half an hour. The island's area is about 270 acres; you can see it all on foot in half a day.

Whether you tour Paquetá on your own or in an excursion group from Rio, you'll enjoy the luxuriant foliage on all sides: tamarinds, acacia, flamboyants, banana plants and fig trees. Most of the island's ten beaches have their own special charms – trees down to the waterline, evocative rock formations or dramatic seascapes. Unfortunately, the waters of Guanabara Bay have become ever more polluted: instead of swimming, you should rent a pedal boat, rowboat or kayak.

King João VI, who built a summer home on Paquetá, called

the island 'A Ilha dos Amores' (The Island of Loves); and honeymooners still make up a high percentage of the clients of the three small hotels. There are slightly more than 3,000 year-round residents, plus the owners of pleasant villas that are mostly occupied during summer. This permanent party is overwhelmed by summer tourists, who arrive at weekends on the thousand-passenger ferries from Praça XV (eight trips a day each way) or on the hydrofoils. Weekdays are less of a crush (and ferry prices are reduced), but the off-season is best of all.

Niterói, which until 1975 was the capital of the state of Rio de Janeiro, is really quite provincial. In an effort to compete with the allure of the city across the bay, far-flung rows of arched bus shelters were erected all along the waterfront, an expensive and aesthetically controversial scheme.

A short taxi or bus ride from the center you come to the small island of **Boa Viagem** (Good Journey), now connected to the Niterói mainland by a footbridge. The island's small white church, built in 1663, perches high above the bay. The island helps to pro- **59**

Just across the bay from Rio, life in Jurujuba seems a world apart.

tect a pleasant semicircular sand beach from the ocean tides. Farther round the coast, more desirable beaches are backed by green hills. Along the coast road the villas snuggle against the hillsides amid palms and hibiscus.

The biggest island in Guanabara Bay, **Ilha do Governador** (Governor's Island), was populated by Indian tribes before the Portuguese colonized it in 1568. In the early 19th century, João VI used to visit the island on hunting expeditions; and Empress Leopoldina established a tiny private zoo here. It was all quite bucolic until about 30 years ago, when a bridge linked Governor's Island to the Rio mainland. Among other rapid developments was the establishment of Galeão International Airport, which has grown to be one of the biggest and best in South America. It employs about 10,000 people. Island residents who work in Rio can commute by hydrofoil – 12 minutes to Praça XV de Novembro, with clean air all the way.

Rio Excursions

Organ Mountains

In January and February, when the sun begins to melt the asphalt streets of Rio, well-to-do Cariocas head for the hills, to the relatively cool climate of the Serra dos Órgãos (Organ Mountains). This has been the fashionable thing to do since the days of the Emperor Pedro II, after whom the town of Petrópolis is named.

Petrópolis is only about 75 kilometers from the center of Rio, but it's a hard drive until you escape the heavy traffic of northern Rio's grim industrial outskirts. Then the scenery along the two roads (one in each direction through the mountains) becomes a wonder of tropical colour: hortensia, hibiscus, bougainvillea, orchids. It is no great surprise to find banana sellers lying in wait along the road; the jungle here is full of banana plants, along with more exotic fruit trees and wild flowers.

The altitude of Petrópolis is 2,750 feet, which all but guarantees a measure of relief from the sea-level heat. But that hardly justifies the German- and Swiss-style chalets of the area. In part they're a fantasy, but they also recall the homesickness of the early colonists, mostly German.

By the second half of the 19th century, all of Rio society wanted to own a villa in Petrópolis, or at least spend the season in one of the town's luxurious hotels. The richly landscaped houses they built, in architectural styles as

Pedro's II's answer to Rio's heat: Petrópolis, upland city of flowers.

unlikely as Norman, Roman and Californian, are among the nicest relics of that golden age. Life in the new 'summer capital' was very relaxing – though not for the emperor, who insisted on wearing his frock coat at all times.

Excursion companies in Rio run half-day tours to Petrópolis; or you can drive yourself (allow two hours each way), or take one of the very frequent express buses from Novo Rio bus station. Less frequent air-conditioned buses operate from the Menezes Cortes bus station on Avenida Erasmo Braga.

However you travel, try to plan your trip in harmony with the schedule of the **Museu Imperial**. Opened in 1945, the museum is housed in the neoclassic Summer

as well as the regalia of the Order of the Garter conferred on him by Queen Victoria. You can also inspect his office, still as it was when he was deposed in 1889.

Another Petrópolis museum, the **Museu Santos Dumont**, commemorates the Brazilian aviation pioneer, a contemporary of the Wright Brothers. In the eccentric three-story Alpine chalet which Dumont built in 1918, many of his personal mementos are now displayed.

The city's **cathedral** looks like a historic building – but it's a case of late-19th-century architects looking back with admiration on French Gothic churches, and it wasn't finished until 1939. Behind a wrought-iron fence are the tombs of Emperor Pedro II and the royal family.

The nicest way to tour Petrópolis is by horse and carriage, which gives you ample time to appreciate the old villas and their gardens. In this city of flowers, it's only natural that the municipal clock tells the time against a background of real flowers. The flowers in the clock (*Relógio de Flores*) at Praça da Liberdade are changed every month.

Continuing some 50 kilometers beyond Petrópolis, you will

Palace, built exactly one century earlier. Noteworthy paintings, tapestries and furniture fill the building, and the floors are so fine that visitors are required to don soft overshoes. The most valuable single exhibit, kept under armed guard, is the imperial crown of Pedro II. With its 639 diamonds and 77 pearls, it weighs more than 3 pounds. Other paraphernalia of power on view include the throne and sword of the emperor, come to another royal retreat, Teresópolis, named after the Empress Teresa Cristina. The annual mean temperature here is a cool 62°F – a dream for sweltering city folk. Some tour companies run full-day excursions combining Petrópolis and Teresópolis.

No single aspect of the town of Teresópolis stands out; it's the springboard for tours of the nearby mountains of the **Parque Nacional da Serra dos Órgãos** (Organ Mountains National Park). Serious alpinists come here to work out on peaks as high as 7,400 feet. The rock formations suggest fanciful names: Mulher de Pedra (Stone Woman), Nariz do Frade (Friar's Nose) and best known of all, visible for many miles around, the slender rock known as the Dedo de Deus (Finger of God).

Another agreeable mountain town, 137 kilometers northeast of Rio de Janeiro, has a peculiar history. **Nova Friburgo** was founded in 1818 by colonists from Switzerland – 1,631 survivors out of more than 2,000 emigrants looking for their Eldorado in Brazil. They were invited, passage paid, by King João VI. Most came from Fribourg (hence the town's name) and the Swiss Jura.

Many of the present-day citizens of Nova Friburgo (population about 90,000), in all the shades of complexion that make up the Brazilian nation, bear names like Balmar, Frossard, Salary and Tinguely; and among the town's hotels are the Sans-Souci, the Hotel dos Alpes and, perhaps unavoidably, Le Chalet Suisse.

Cabo Frio

If you own a yacht, Cabot Frio is an ideal place to keep it. There are several yacht clubs, but best of all is to build a house on the waterfront and tie up your boat outside. Along the banks of the wide channels linking the center of Cabo Frio with the open Atlantic are hundreds of luxurious villas, many of them beautifully landscaped, with their own piers or ramps. Boat trips around Cabo Frio entail the same kind of commentary as a Hollywood rubberneck tour. The guide calls out the names and titles of the owners of the houses along the way (São Paulo magnates and Rio TV and

At Arraial do Cabo, 100 miles from Rio: a beach to dream of.

movie stars), while the tourists snap pictures of the celebrities sunbathing on their lawns.

Some 150 kilometers east of Rio, Cabo Frio is a resort town of notable contrasts: yachtsmen and fishermen, the heart-warming flowering trees and the unexpected abundance of tall spiky cactus, green gardens and vivid white dunes. At the main quay, under the low-hanging coconut palms, hippie-style entrepreneurs peddle jewelry, dolls and toys to tourists of all types.

The famous navigator Amerigo Vespucci, who gave his name to the continent, is credited with discovering Cabo Frio in 1503. He called it 'Cold Cape' not because of the wind but because the sea water was particularly cold. The earliest and most intriguing

Original fashions and jewelry on sale at Cabo Frio quay, where the sightseeing boats depart.

building standing in Cabo Frio is **Forte de São Mateus** (St Matthew's Fort), an outpost founded in 1616 and proudly preserved. The fort is said to have been erected by the French when Cabo Frio was still a free-for-all of Portuguese, Dutch, English and French expeditions hunting brazilwood and spices.

The most modish resort on the coast, **Búzios**, is situated 18 kilometers northeast of Cabo Frio. Like St Tropez, it's a fishing village that suddenly won the hearts of the jet set, and hotels and inns began to sprout. Low white houses, resplendent vegetation, and endless curving sand beaches are just about the whole story. Pioneering tourists themselves give Búzios that intangible 'extra' which busloads of more-or-less ordinary citizens come to see. The area has excellent fishing and is a favorite spot for diving.

The trip between this area of the so-called Sun Coast and metropolitan Rio offers many visual surprises and pleasures: salt pans with windmills, miles of unspoiled beaches fringing clean, calm seas, and a backdrop of voluptuously curved green hills, some with orchards of orange trees planted in military ranks.

Brasília

With its futuristic city plan of handsome glass palaces and self-contained apartment villages, Brasília makes a fascinating destination for anyone interested in architecture or urban development. Fresh air and a sky larger than life enhance this peek into the 21st century. Thanks to intensive airline connections, the capital is within easy reach of Rio, but an overnight stay is needed.

As recently as the 1950s, all was wilderness on this plateau halfway between the Amazon jungle and the fleshpots of Rio. Brazil's equivalent of a space program opened a new frontier and changed the nation's center of gravity.

The visionary plan moved from rough sketches to steel and concrete in record time. But problems arose that no one had anticipated, marring the reality of what had been a theoretical utopia. The energy-conservation situation brought into question Brasília's reliance on cars: nothing is within walking distance. And because of massive migration to the new capital, the district's population has already swollen to double the size pro- **67** jected for the end of the century. All of which has strained municipal services and imposed some adjustments and compromises onto the idealistic pilot plan. They've even had to install a few traffic lights, hitherto deemed superfluous in such a brilliantly planned highway network.

The road from theory to Brasília was so long and difficult that the crash program of construction seems even more of a whirlwind than it actually was. The capital of the country had always been on the coast – first at Bahia, then Rio – but for more than two centuries Brazilian philosophers had been advocating a move inland as the only way to develop the whole of the country. In 1891 the Republic's new constitution officially vowed to move the capital, someday, to the central plateau. Feasibility studies, committee reports and decrees nudged the program toward Brasília, but the time for action didn't arrive until 1956. President Juscelino Kubitschek won unanimous parliamentary approval for his bill creating a bureaucracy empowered to plan and actually construct the new city. 'JK', as he was known, gave city planners *carte blanche*.

Before the city could be built, a measure of civilization had to be implanted on the plateau, about 3,600 feet above sea level, formerly the home of a few free-ranging cattle and scrubby trees. There were no roads, railways, electricity, telephones, or water or sewage lines. For the pioneers it was a muddy (or dusty, according to the season) grind, full of sacrifices warmed by hope, with overtones of the Wild West.

Brazil's greatest architect, Oscar Niemeyer, was put in charge of designing the buildings. The urbanist Lúcio Costa won a competition to draw up the grand design for a city for people, and landscape architect Roberto Burle Marx was commissioned to bring life to the spaces between the monuments.

Four years later, when the government was transferred to Brasília, the city was still so unfinished and rugged that bureaucrats and foreign diplomats had to be coerced to abandon the high-life of Rio and move to the plateau. Then they complained about the provincial nightlife – which has since become more invigorated – and the vagaries of shopping under a decentralized urban scheme that has no 'downtown'. Even pessimists who live in the area of the pilot plan count themselves very lucky. Hundreds of thousands more – the overflow – have to live in satellite cities that are at best uninspiring. The commuters now outnumber the residents of the model city.

An 'Air Bridge' (*Ponte Aérea*) – run jointly by several domestic airlines – offers about 18 flights a day in each direction between Rio's international airport and Brasília. In practice it's wise to make a reservation in advance. On-board service during the 80-minute jet flight ranges from good to excellent. Brasília's climate is milder than Rio's. The rainy season runs from November to March, providing some spectacular cloud assemblies for photographers. You can see the highlights of Brazil's capital in a day, but don't set out on foot. The distances are just too great.

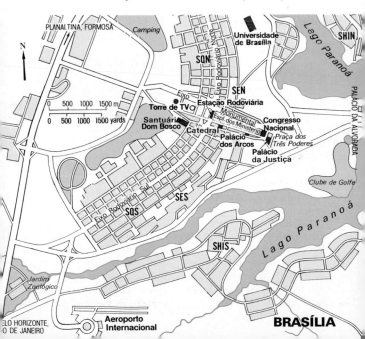

What to See

Lúcio Costa's conception of Brasília began as a simple cross on a piece of paper and evolved into a curved axis crossing a straight line, like the wings and fuselage of an airplane. The straight line – which is called the **Eixo Monumental** (Monumental Axis) – is the area set aside for government and culture. The intersecting arc, called the **Eixo Rodoviário** (Highway Axis), neatly slices through the capital's residential districts, divided into 'superblocks' that are self-sufficient mini-neighborhoods. The 'wings' and 'body' intersect – on separate levels, for Brasília does not have any old-fashioned street crossings – at the Bus Terminal (Estação Rodoviária), around which the city's business and entertainment facilities are located.

On the way in from the airport (15 minutes to the exact center of town) excursion leaders or taxi-driver-guides explain the lay of the land and the initially confusing road signs. Brasilienses (residents of the capital) have to know dozens of abbreviations and acronyms: SHIN means North Individual Housing Sector, for example, and SQS means Super-quadra Sul (South Superblock).

Tourists are taken through a typical superblock, with its own recreational and shopping facilities and school. They visit one of the simple churches built in the pioneer days, then the impressive **Santuário Dom Bosco**, a church with tall pointed-arch windows composed of small squares of heavenly blue glass. Later on the agenda is Brasília's **cathedral** – actually far bigger than it looks

Oscar Niemeyer's sweeping arcs grace Brasília's Congress. The wide open spaces of the urban plan remain, but the population has soared.

since only the cupola is above ground. The gracefully curved struts of its conical superstructure form one of the capital's principal landmarks. Inside, natural sunlight cheers (and sometimes overheats) the circular nave. Three large aluminum angels float near the ceiling, adding to the airy charm of a thoroughly unconventional church.

The cathedral is beside the Monumental Axis, which leads to the area of the **Esplanada dos Ministérios**, with each ministry in its own identical, rather Kafkaesque, glass box. Students of government will not be surprised to learn that all the ministries have outgrown their headquarters – so luxurious new annexes have been built to accommodate the swarms of additional public servants.

At the far end of the Monumental Axis, the **Praça dos Três Poderes** (Plaza of the Three Powers) witnesses the confrontation, or convergence, of the executive, legislative and judicial branches of the federal government. The architecture here reaches its apex, as if each of the Three Powers were striving to achieve the most beautiful or original symbol.

Dominating the entire ensemble is the **Congresso Nacional** (Congress), noted for the counterpoint of its dome and inverted dome – the only visible parts of the subterranean chambers of the

Sellers of dried flowers near Brasília's cathedral. The spiked cupola disguises the true size of the church, which is mostly below ground.

House of Representatives and the Federal Senate. Between these halls rise twin 28-story administrative towers. The zoning laws assure that no building in Brasília will ever be taller. Behind the complex, swans glide around a grand pool sometimes squabbling almost as heatedly as the lawmakers inside.

An impressive group of **sculptures** stands in the great plaza. The best-known monument is dedicated to the Candangos, the people who came here to build the new capital. And notice the serene modern version of Justice blindfolded, sitting before the Palácio da Justica (Supreme Court). Another greatly admired sculpture is the powerful work called *The Meteor*, by Bruno Giorgi, in the lotus pool in front of the lavish **Palácio dos Arcos** (Palace of the Arches). The building – also known as Palácio do Itamaraty – is used for diplomatic receptions, so the decor and furnishings are most elegant. To visit you must apply for permission 24 hours in advance.

Of all Brasília's palaces, the long, low **Palácio da Alvorada** (Palace of the Dawn) is the least pompous and most human. Oscar Niemeyer is reputed to have de-signed its upside-down arches in a single night, and Kubitschek hailed the building's 'lightness, grandeur, lyricism and majesty'. The palace, which serves as the presidential residence, is on the shore of a man-made lake, called Lago Paranoá, that has a perimeter of 50 miles. It brightens the scenery and gives the landlocked Brasilienses a welcome chance to do some boating and fishing.

Also overlooking the lake are **Embassy Sectors North and South** (SEN and SES). Here architects from various countries tried to express the very best in national traditions or trends. No two buildings are alike, and some are truly inspired. You'll also want to admire the luxurious private homes near the lake shore.

To put Brasília into perspective, be sure to take the elevator to the observation level of the **Torre de TV** *(Television Tower)* and see how the city fits into the encircling plain. Here and there you'll notice an excavation site with the red earth visible like a wound in what's now such a green, tidy parkland. And from very near the center of the pilot plan, you'll be able to judge how it all grew from a simple cross on a piece of paper.

What to Do

Carnival

Rio's annual explosion of music, color and joy is even bigger and better than you could possibly imagine. The Carioca Carnival surpasses all other pageants and festivals in the world. Even Hollywood, with the biggest budget in history, couldn't produce such a breathtaking spectacle.

More than half a million people, all in costume, march, dance and sing in the organized parades. Other revels, in and out of fancy dress, involve thousands more. And for high society and many tourists, the fashionable masquerade balls provide unforgettable diversion to climax the frenzy of the holiday.

Carnival is so all-pervasive that even if you boycotted the hundreds of special events scattered around town, you couldn't walk a hundred yards from your hotel without bumping into a spontaneous party in the street. Whether the music is performed by neighborhood children with makeshift snare drums or a band of polished musicians, the samba is hopelessly contagious.

In Rio, the last fling before the austere Lenten season starts in earnest the Friday before Shrove Tuesday (Mardi Gras). It goes on for five days and five nights – more than 100 hours of almost nonstop frolics.

Until the middle of the 19th century, Carnival in Rio was an aimless and often unseemly outbreak of water fights and practical jokes, derived from Portuguese tradition. In 1855, a band of young men donned colorful costumes and marched to music. As the idea caught fire with the public, other groups were formed and special marches were composed for the bands. Soon the music evolved into the Brazilian form of light-hearted *choros* and sombre *ranchos*. After World War I, the pace picked up with the invention of the samba, and the groups of revelers became bigger and better disciplined.

The modern era began in 1928 with the organization of the first *escola de samba* (samba school) – not a school at all, but a confraternity of Carnival celebrants

The parade before the judges is the climax of a year's work for fanatics of Rio's samba schools.

74

united in their dedication to perfecting the music, dancing, costumes and floats. Several more *escolas* soon followed, and by 1933 a formal jury had been set up to choose the best group in the parade. Ever since, the competition for Carnival honors has been as exciting to the Cariocas as the World Series to North Americans – but much more controversial.

Mounting Excitement

For weeks before the holiday, you can feel the excitement sweeping over the city as local enthusiasts rehearse for Carnival out on the street. The drummers beat their hearts out for the director, who cues them with a police whistle. The rhythm is as precise as a machine, as catchy as a virus.

On the Friday before Shrove Tuesday, flimsy kiosks suddenly appear on street corners, selling last-minute costume-party ideas: Hawaiian leis made of paper, children's horror masks, plastic noisemakers, paper streamers, confetti. Along the Avenida Rio Branco, normally a sober street of banks and prestige business offices, the cheerful decorations are up and workmen are busy covering the show windows with temporary wooden defenses. The sound and fury of the first parades will concentrate here, and nobody underestimates the force of a crowd in motion.

In the evening, a little behind schedule, the Carnival king and queen receive the key to the city. From the edge of the crowd, the queen in her revealing costume looks unbelievably beautiful. The surprising thing is that she looks just as good up close. The police allow the crowd to mill around her admiringly; they're only worried about pickpockets.

And then the first Carnival club parades past – hundreds of dancers, singers and drummers thumping a dozen different kinds of percussion instruments. Amid all the brilliantly costumed marchers are fantasy floats pulled by tow trucks or pushed by unsung volunteers. The tourists in the crowd cheer and tap their feet to the music, but the Cariocas are strangely restrained. They know this is still minor-league play; the champions of samba won't show themselves for another two days.

On the Saturday night, the parades take place in half a dozen locations. At the main site, the Passarela do Samba stadium, grandstands and V.I.P. viewing booths have been erected at a cost of millions of dollars. All the tickets have been sold (and often resold at considerable profit), but your hotel can find a way to procure an expensive ticket for you. Since the major *escolas* are still waiting in the wings, the Saturday night is in the nature of a rehearsal for the TV crews, police and soft-drink salesmen. Nevertheless, for the tourists the parade is eye-popping.

Vast armies of girls and boys, women and men, in the most outlandish and imaginative costumes dance, strut or march past the stands, at about one mile per hour. Each *bloco* of about two to three thousand members has its own costume designs, floats (called *alegorias*), song and dance. It can take an hour or more for one whole team to pass and another half hour to prepare the next *bloco*, so the program continues far beyond Sunday's sunrise. You'll discover the secret of the endurance of paraders, officials and bystanders: hidden reserves of energy seem to surface at the sound of the samba.

The most exciting *escolas de samba* parade in two halves – one on Sunday and one on Monday – through the superb Passarela do Samba stadium, or Sambadrome. If the elegant structure reminds you of Brasília, it's because it was designed by Oscar Niemeyer, the architect of many of Brasíl buildings. Packed into the st which have replaced the bleachers erected ever Marquês de Sapuca dances and sing members of ea into thirty to toons call as Indian braves, 18th-century lords and ladies, pirates, fairies, caliphs, harlequins, mandarins, clowns, animals, ballet dancers and spear-carriers. The girls wear more peacock and ostrich feathers than you'll see in the zoo, and enough tinsel and rhinestones to stun you. The floats are clever, original and complicated. Many of them are decorated with girls, who wave to the crowd, dance or just look beautiful.

Each *escola de samba* chooses a theme (*enredo*) for itself, which it illustrates with music and color. Carnival chronicler Luís Gardel wrote that each of the productions

is 'a peripatetic grand opera, with soloists, prima donnas, chorus, corps de ballet, orchestra, scenery and apotheosis – conceived, created, put together and produced by people of very modest means, not a few of them illiterates, but who are endowed with a natural gift for the arts.'

The requirements of tradition and drama have mostly standardized the order of march and the general content of each *escola*'s production. A float setting the theme appears first, followed by a small group of dignified gentlemen – the officials of the *escola* (*comissão de frente*) – who salute the jury and the audience. Other obligatory elements include at least one group of young dancers (sometimes these are small children), as well as a beautiful standard-bearer (*porta-bandeira*) and her fast-dancing escort, both usually wearing 18th-century finery. Young ladies in elaborate costumes, often sheltering under parasols, are followed by considerably older ladies – some of advanced age – dressed as Baianas, women of Bahia.

Somewhere in the first half of the parade marches the *bateria*, the band of amazingly varied and eloquent percussion instruments. And then there are more floats, dancers and beautiful *mulatas* moving as sensually as cabaret stars. Everyone in the cast, including the roving platoon leaders who keep them on their toes, is gleefully singing the samba school's own samba in perfect time to the drums, mostly in tune, 79 without a break for the hour it takes to move from the beginning to the finish line. Thousands in the audience have also learned the tune and most of the words. They join in the choruses, dancing in the stands.

Parades go on day and night at several other places, but they are less exciting to the crowds than Sunday and Monday's battle for samba-school supremacy. All the *escolas* are severely judged, on criteria ranging from rhythm and harmony to choreography, timing and overall motion. The official results, which detonate heated joy, despair and controversy all over Rio, are announced the following Thursday. Two days later, all the winners parade before enthusiastic crowds.

Fancy Dress Balls
Ten days before Mardi Gras, the social season moves into top gear with the first of scores of dances. Many clubs and organizations in Rio sponsor Carnival balls, with tickets normally on sale to the public; some clubs give as many as five different dances, as well as a couple of children's parties.

At the chic parties, evening dress or 'luxurious fantasy costumes' are specified. In practice, nobody expects a tourist to pack a tuxedo or buy expensive masquerade gear, but a bit of effort is appreciated. It's cheap and easy to improvise a costume – for instance a Hawaiian shirt and some paper leis. The locals are expected to dress more lavishly and wittily, and they do.

The smart parties cost far more than a normal night on the town, as you'd expect. A buffet is usually included in the price, but drinks can be a serious extra expense. Hotel porters have private supply lines to hard-to-get tickets and can give advice on costume requirements and transportation.

The glamorous and funny costumes, the decorations, the music and the lusty enthusiasm of the participants make carnival balls outstanding parties by any standards. If you're not up to a long night's bash, it's still worth waiting at the entrance to one of the clubs to watch the costumed revelers arriving or (if you're up early) departing. The local tourist authorities and newspapers issue complete lists of the major balls, as well as all the parades.

Surviving Carnival
Every year the newspapers report an appalling toll of dead and in-

jured during Carnival time. This should cause no alarm: about as many victims would have suffered accidents in a normal five-day period. But the chances of running into a drunk driver during Carnival, or vice-versa, is much less far-fetched; so be very careful when driving or walking. Since crime takes no holiday, it would be foolhardy to go out on the town wearing ostentatious jewelry or carrying more money than absolutely essential.

And then there are 'Carnival romances'. You can dance with anybody at the Carnival balls, but the smiles and flirtatious gestures of the Brazilian girls should not necessarily be taken at face value. Brazilian men are jealous in a very old-fashioned way; fights can and do break out. Discretion can be a life-saver.

On a more mundane level, take some sandwiches and cushions for the long nights of parades at the Passarela do Samba stadium. People in the viewing stands are cut off from the itinerant snack salesmen and hot-dog emporia found in abundance outside the gates. Soft drinks, on the other hand, are readily available.

If, as the meteorological odds strongly suggest, it should rain some of the time during Carnival, join the Cariocas in ignoring the problem. Under umbrellas, or bareheaded and soaked, they keep dancing, singing and laughing. The only noticeable change in the program is the universal rainy-day nuisance: taxis suddenly become hard to find. The city's buses, however, never stop running during the holiday period.

Though banks and many offices are closed for the long weekend, essential services are maintained. Restaurants and snack bars tend to operate normally, and neighborhood shops are open much of the time for last-minute necessities. But don't expect Rio to run with cool efficiency during Carnival. The hotel maid who forgot to make your bed may be recovering from a hangover.

Finally, if you can't take the frantic Carnival tempo, you're not alone. Hundreds of thousands of Cariocas head for the hills every year to avoid the noise and the mobs. But by far the quietest alternative is offered by the Archdiocese of Rio, which runs a religious retreat during Carnival. Every year hundreds attend this devout anti-Carnival, while all around the crowds roar.

Other Festivals and Folklore

Afro-Brazilian traditions fuel the most vivid events in the life of Rio de Janeiro. A powerful element is the mystic faith which arrived with the African slaves and coexists remarkably with Christianity. Converted slaves found it convenient to light a candle in church for St Jerome, for example, while actually intending it for the saint's African counterpart, Xangô. The equivalent of Jesus is the deity Oxalá.

Every January 20 in Rio, two holidays are celebrated. The Catholic festival of St Sebastian, at the cathedral, honors the city's patron saint; and a parallel festival honors the saint's equivalent, Oxóssi, the god of the forest.

The mystical *umbanda* rites – also known as *macumba* – follow a complicated liturgical calendar, which varies from city to city in different parts of Brazil. One holiday in Rio occurs on December 31, a date easy to remember, when priests and priestesses and their followers gather on the beaches with candles and flowers in homage to Iemanjá, the goddess of the sea. It's a strangely moving ceremony to watch.

Another seaside festival takes place in late June, when Rio's fishermen honor St Peter, their patron saint. There are seaborne processions, and ceremonies are held ashore in Urca.

One of the year's biggest *festas* is a combined religious and popular festival every Sunday in October at Igreja de Penha in

The effigy indicates the sale of items used in umbanda *rituals.*

North Rio. Cariocas celebrate with plenty of music, food and drink at the Festa da Penha.

On the year's most solemn holiday, Good Friday, actors in biblical-era costumes proceed through the city retracing the events of the Way of the Cross.

The municipal tourism organization, Riotur, issues an annual calendar of events of interest to visitors, as well as monthly pamphlets providing later and fuller details of all major holidays, fairs, festivals and special happenings.

One aspect of folklore you'll probably enjoy in Rio is *capoeira*. If you don't see it in a nightclub, you'll bump into it at a marketplace or in a busy square. *Capoeira* is an Afro-Brazilian form of combat which looks like a cross between a dance and acrobatics. While attendants beat drums and coax the sounds from single-stringed musical instruments called *berimbaus*, the fighters perform delicate handsprings and other feats according to rules that are as arcane as those of kung fu. Street-corner demonstrations are a mild souvenir of the oldtime *capoeira*, which was outlawed in 1890 because criminal gangs used it to keep the police off balance.

Nightlife

Rio de Janeiro is a town for night people, with plenty of action going on as late as you like in big brassy nightclubs and friendly piano bars, in chic discos and dark, smoky *'boates'*. Whether you're watching, listening or dancing, the emphasis is on the samba. The beat gets to the heart – and feet – of just about everyone, sooner or later.

Now for the bad news. A recent survey of two dozen important cities revealed that a bottle of Scotch cost more in Rio than anywhere else in the civilized world. Fortunately, the alternatives are many, from the humble but unexcelled local draft beer to Brazilian liqueurs. There's even a native fizzy wine that's patterned after champagne.

Clubs with elaborate shows inflict cover or minimum charges, or both. But the well-known spots give value for money, as the presence of local clients indicates.

Some clubs concentrate on the samba, with big orchestras and vibrant dancers in spangles and feathers. Others have frankly erotic shows in which striptease is only the overture. A third type specializes in Brazilian folklore,

including simulations of *umbanda* rites. Others attract customers with good music and bad girls. For an unusual night out, try a *gafieira* or dance hall, where ordinary Cariocas go to let off steam.

For less frivolous visitors, there are legitimate theaters and cinemas. Plays, the vast majority by contemporary Brazilian playwrights, are presented in Portuguese. Foreign films are normally shown with the original dialogue, Portuguese subtitles being added.

The season for concerts and recitals, with celebrated foreign artists, lasts from about March to November, which is also the opera season at Rio's plush Teatro Municipal.

The newspapers *Jornal do Brasil* and *o Globo* publish two or three pages daily tabulating entertainment in Rio.

Shopping

Gemstones are the glittering prospect for shoppers in Rio. They don't grow on trees, but they're sold at encouraging prices all over town – in hotel boutiques, in downtown stores and on street corners by contrabandists with pockets full of emeralds … or almost-emeralds. Only Russia is said to outstrip Brazil in the production of precious stones; but that doesn't allow for the estimated U.S. $100,000,000 a year in stones smuggled out of Brazil or otherwise unaccounted for.

The most popular buys are amethysts, aquamarines, opals, topazes and tourmalines. But diamonds, emeralds, rubies and sapphires are also mined in Brazil. Stones can be bought uncut, cut but not set, or made up into rings, pendants or bracelets. (For American citizens planning major purchases, the U.S. Consulate issues a pamphlet summarizing the latest customs regulations.)

Other shopping ideas in brief:

Antiques. Colonial-era religious statuettes and ceremonial swords, and painted tiles.

Art. The gallery scene is very lively; the monthly Riotur pamphlets list the major shows.

Batik prints of Brazilian folklore themes.

Butterflies and moths of exquisite markings and colors, once alive, now preserved under glass.

Coffee. You'll never be closer to the source. Carry-aboard cartons are sold at the airport.

Dolls, especially in Bahia costumes with colorful hats.

Figas. The Brazilian fist symbol with the thumb pointing out, in many materials and sizes from bracelet charm to paperweight.

Hammocks. To re-create the tropical pace in your own garden.

Indian products. Blowpipes, spears, tomahawks and jewelry from northern Brazilian tribes.

Jacaranda wood salad bowls and trays.

Kites, made of cloth, in fighting-bird shape and bright colors.

Leather. Bags, belts, wallets and shoes.

Musical instruments. Flutes and the wonderful percussion instruments of Carnival fame.

Plants. The miraculous *pau d'água* – which looks like a dead stick, but flourishes with the addition of water.

Recordings (discs and tapes) of sambas, boss nova tunes and folk music.

Straw bags, baskets and hats.

Swimsuits. If they're not too daring for your nearest beach, a showy souvenir of Rio.

Where to Shop
The most sophisticated boutiques are in Ipanema. Copacabana has more variety, except for clothing, and prices there are generally a bit lower. Other good bets are the pedestrian area in Rio's business center and Botafogo's Rio-Sul shopping center.

Fairs and Markets
All over Rio de Janeiro street markets specializing in fresh foods provide a lively free show, usually once a week in each neighbourhood. Take your camera for the brilliantly colored fruits, vegetables and flowers, as well as the 'characters' selling and buying with much intensity.

On weekends, several fairs or markets of more specific tourist interest are scheduled. Even the calculated 'art fairs' have a lot to offer the visitor.

Feira do Nordeste. This is by far the most exotic and memorable of all the markets, with thousands of buyers and sellers in a scene calling to mind a Middle-Eastern bazaar. The address is Campo de São Cristóvão in the Northern Zone of Rio; take any bus marked São Cristóvão.

Every Sunday, from 6 am until 1 pm, you can watch dancers and musicians, faith healers, patent-medicine demonstrators and sellers of tropical fish, holy pictures, spices and rumpled clothing. You can also sample authentic food

On sale at a Sunday fair: lizards (a useful element in Brazilian folk remedies) and religious art.

from northeastern Brazil, or have your shoes or watch repaired.

Notice the stands with pamphlets hung on strings – called *Literatura de Cordel*, or cord literature – whose authors recite or sing their works to encourage sales. The rhymed stories, often based on true events, have titles like 'The Husband Who Traded His Wife for a Bottle of Hootch'.

Feirarte. This busy art fair occupies Praça General Osório in Ipanema every Sunday from 9 am to 6 pm. Local painters display the sort of canvases you'd find in New York's Greenwich Village or London's Piccadilly, as well as native motifs. Leatherwork, carvings, tapestries and jewelry round out the show.

Feirarte 11. All day Thursday and Friday the historic Praça XV de Novembro is given over to this fair, similar to that of any small town. Craftsmen sell dolls, jewelry, embroidery, leather goods and musical instruments. Sidewalk artists will sketch your portrait while you wait. Booths selling Bahian food add to the color.

Feira de Antiquários. This antiques market, scheduled for 8 am to 5 pm on Saturdays at Praça Marechal Âncora (near Praça XV de Novembro), has well-organized stands where you may spot old Chinese sculptures or Portuguese tiles, a 19th-century pistol or a vintage camera.

Feira de Trocas. 'Bargain Fair' is the official translation for this market, where nothing is bought or sold, only traded. This, too, is a Saturday affair, at Cais Pharoux, opposite Praça XV de Novembro. The only chance of finding something worth having in this pile of junk is the off-chance that a trader doesn't realize he owns a collectible antique (perhaps a first-generation transistor radio or 78-rpm records) – but you have to offer him an item he wants to collect, in return.

Sports

The first thing most people want to do when they arrive in Rio is dive into the surf. No problem. There are beaches to meet all requirements, from appealing crescents of gradually sloping sand to wide open spaces under almost constant attack by the sea. For a rundown on what to expect all along the coast, see pp. 40–45.

Remember that this is the At-

lantic, subject to tricky tides and changes of mood. Appearances are often deceptive; an apparently mild beach may suffer a raging undertow. So if the lifeguard hoists a red flag, stay out of the water, no matter how inviting it looks. And children should never be permitted to swim unattended.

Water Sports
Surfing. After a long battle for recognition, Rio's surfers won the right-of-way at Arpoador beach, next to Ipanema. Farther down the coast, almost anywhere the waves are running, they take matters into their own hands.

Windsurfing. After a difficult start, the well-balanced sport of windsurfing has caught a belated blast of enthusiasm from Cariocas. Sales of these very expensive rigs are booming, but at last report none was available for rent. In this new field, the situation

could change rapidly, so check with one of the firms selling the equipment or teaching the sport.

Fishing. Shops all over town sell fishing tackle. You'll find experienced fishermen working the cliffs along Avenida Niemeyer or casting from beaches.

Deep-sea fishermen must be ready for a little traveling. The tuna, marlin and dorado tend to stay out at the continental shelf, about 40 miles from Rio. The best time of year is October to December. Trips can be arranged through the Bateau Mouche organization. Other boats from 14 to 42 feet can be chartered from various owners based at the Marina da Glória.

Scuba diving. Local underwater fishermen find challenging sport around several Atlantic islands, including the ones directly off Ipanema – the Cagarras and, twice as distant, the Ilha Redonda. For information about boat hire, check the port alongside the Yacht Club in Urca. To find out about about scuba-diving equipment, look in the classified telephone directory (yellow pages) under 'Caça submarina', or go to the Marina da Glória.

Yachting. Unless you are a member of the Rio Yacht Club, or entered in one of the regattas (every weekend from March through December), this may well have to be a spectator sport. But you might try to rent a boat at the Marina da Glória.

Sports Ashore

Golf. Both of Rio's golf courses allow visitors to play, subject to certain restrictions. For information, inquire at the Itanhangá Golf Club or the Gávea Golf Club. At each of these courses, caddies and clubs are available.

Tennis. The big new hotels on the Vidigal–São Conrado beaches have their own courts; or if you're staying elsewhere, you might ask your hotel desk clerk to make arrangements with the Rio Country Club.

Public tennis facilities are extremely limited.

Sports Aloft

Hang gliding. Tourists with credentials and their own wings can join the local pilots riding the breezes from Pedra Bonita, above São Conrado. (Hang gliding in Portuguese is *vôo livre*.)

Parachute jumping. See the Clube Olimpo, at 58 Avenida Ernâni Cardoso, for information regarding equipment and jumps, which generally take place on Saturday and Sunday mornings.

Spectator Sports

Soccer (football). In Rio, it's not just how the game is played, but how much fun the fans have – with their firecrackers, banners, music and all-round good spirits. Headline-writers abbreviate two of the principal teams 'Fla" and 'Flu", for Flamengo and Fluminense, but nothing else is confusing. (The other leading local clubs are América and Vasco da Gama.) At the Maracanã stadium (see p. 54) you can watch virtuoso soccer in a happy, enthusiastic environment. The big games usually take place on Sundays.

Horse racing. All the buses marked 'Via Joquei' (meaning Jockey Club) pass the Hipódromo da Gávea, which occupies a large, pleasant chunk of land reclaimed from the lagoon. Races are held on Saturday and Sunday afternoons and on Monday and Thursday evenings. The Jockey Club's biggest sporting and social event of the year is the competition for the Grande Prêmio Brasil in August.

Car racing. The Autódromo da Cidade do Rio de Janeiro, which occupies more than 200 acres in Jacarepaguá., can accommodate up to 65,000 fans for international races.

Dining in Rio

In the melting pot of Brazil, three totally different concepts of a square meal have interacted delectably. The Indians, who were here first, contributed vegetables, grains and an appreciation of the abundant local seafood. The Portuguese, who colonized Brazil, brought their stews and sweet tooth. Then the African slaves they imported added new spices and sauces in turn.

Later immigrants introduced novelties from other nationalities: knackwurst, pizzas and hamburgers are fully assimilated by now. Brazil is a big country, with food to match. Whatever the recipe or its derivation, the raw materials couldn't be more auspicious.

Brazil is one of the world's leading cattle-rearing countries, so the meat is first-class and relatively inexpensive. The South Atlantic provides a bonanza of fish and seafood. In the tropics, familiar fruits and vegetables are juicier than ever – and unfamiliar ones excite the adventurous palate.

You may not agree with the contention that Brazilian cooking is in the same class as French or Chinese cuisine for originality and grandeur. But you'll certain-

ly be glad to have made the acquaintance of Brazil's array of wholesome and fascinating food.

Choosing a Restaurant

In Rio it's easy to find the right restaurant for your mood and appetite: a fish house on the beach or a candlelit French restaurant, a bohemian pasta parlor or a barbecue with waiters in Gaucho costumes. To find out what's going on in any restaurant, just look in the window – though in many cases there's no window at all, only tables overflowing onto the sidewalk. Restaurants post their menus beside the door, so you know the price range and specialties in advance.

Most tourists stay at Zona Sul beaches and therefore quite logically take advantage of the many good restaurants nearby. But it's also worth exploring the central business district, which boasts a distinguished roster of French, German, Portuguese, Spanish and even Brazilian restaurants.

When to Eat

Hotels usually include breakfast (*café da manhã*) in the price of the room – fresh fruit juice, toast and rolls, butter, marmalade, and coffee with hot milk. The hours are posted, generally 7 to 9 or 10 am. If you miss breakfast, you can catch up at a stand-up street-corner café. However, the city's relaxing sidewalk cafés don't normally serve breakfast.

Meal times for both lunch and dinner are uncommonly flexible. Lunch (*almoço*) can start at 11.30 or 12, or more fashionably at 1 or 2 pm, and go on as long as you please. Dinner (*jantar*) can begin as early as 7.30 or 8 pm, but many restaurants stay open until 1, 2 or 3 am, or until the last customer goes home. Most restaurants are open seven days a week.

Brazilian Cuisine

The national dish of Brazil, *feijoada*, contains 18 or 19 ingredients and takes hours to prepare. It also takes hours to digest, which is why you'd be wise not to order it at night. Most Cariocas eat it at lunch on Saturday, then take the rest of the day to recover.

If you like unusual combinations of tastes and textures, you'll rave about *feijoada*. This typically Carioca stew is a feast of black beans with sausage and other pork products and dried beef, flavored with onions, garlic, chives, tomato, parsley and perhaps hot peppers, then served with boiled

rice, cassava flour, shredded kale and – a brilliant afterthought – fresh slices of orange. It's almost obligatory to start or accompany this meal with a *batida*, a Brazilian rum sour. Discreet *feijoada* fanciers follow this with nothing stronger than mineral water.

From Brazil's southernmost state of Rio Grande do Sul comes the cowboy food, *churrasco*. Cariocas and tourists alike enjoy

In Gaucho fashion, meat sizzles over charcoal at a churrascaria.

dining at *churrascarias*, which serve barbecued meat in the Gaucho style. Strips of beef, plus sausages, chicken or chops, are skewered and roasted over charcoal. Authentically the meat has to be kept moist with brine, and the spit is inclined at a 45-degree **95** angle over the fire. A very popular species of *churrascaria* advertises the *rodízio* system. For a fixed price, you get to eat as much as you want of all the barbecues in the house. The waiters arrive with one skewer after another, tempting you first with a sausage, then a chop, then a chunk of steak, then a lamb cutlet… You don't have to know the language, but you certainly need a formidable appetite.

The state of Minas Gerais, north of Rio, provides an exquisite dish that would be worth ordering for its name alone: *tutú*. A thoroughly prosaic translation would be black-bean mush. But bean-lovers think *tutú* is too tasty to be true, being a subtle mixture of beans, bacon and sausage or

The relaxed tropical elegance of a Copacabana restaurant.

jerked beef, manioc meal and onion, usually served with shredded kale and hard-boiled egg.

Brazil's foremost contributions to the art of cooking come from the northeast, where the Indian, African and European currents meet. Rio has several good restaurants specializing in these spicy delights. Here are three of many celebrated dishes:

Acarajé. A large fritter made from a batter of ground beans,

deep-fried in boiling *dendê* oil, the yellowish palm oil indispensable to Bahian cooking. The resultant dumpling is split down the middle and liberally filled with *vatapá* (see below), dried shrimp and hot *malagueta* pepper sauce. It is served as a starter or snack.

Vatapá. This Bahian specialty calls to mind shrimp creole, but it's more complicated, with subtly interacting flavors. The ingredients may include shrimp, fish, grated coconut, ground peanuts, cashew nuts, tomato, onion, hot pepper, ginger, coriander, olive oil, *dendê* oil, pepper and salt. This is thickened with bread crumbs and served with rice cooked in coconut milk.

Xinxim (pronounced shing-SHING) – another name to inspire the imagination – is a chicken stew from Bahia. What makes it different from all other chicken-in-the-pot recipes is the addition of ground dried shrimp and the use of hot spices and *dendê* oil. Approach the hot sauce served on the side with caution!

Seafood Restaurants
Many Rio restaurants deal primarily in fish and seafood, often prepared according to Portuguese or Spanish recipes. As elsewhere, **97**

the price levied for lobster (actually crayfish or spiny lobster) could embarrass your budget. But other shellfish are within reasonable reach. Look for *zarzuela de mariscos*, a thick Spanish version of a *bouillabaisse*, or the Portuguese variants, *caldeirada* or *frutos do mar ensopados*.

Generally, when they eat fish, Cariocas prefer a thick fillet, as they are nervous about fishbones. So in many restaurants you'll find dishes described vaguely as *filet de peixe* (fish fillet). The fish in question often turns out to be *badejo* (bass), tasty in spite of its anonymity, but sometimes over-whelmed by a thick sauce. You can also get excellent sole (*linguado*). The sauce called *belle meunière* is a butter sauce complicated, with typical Brazilian enthusiasm, by the addition of shrimp, mushrooms, asparagus, capers and whatever else will make it seem luxurious. In the Portuguese restaurants, you can choose from many varieties of *bacalhau*, dried salt cod, usually baked in a rich sauce.

Hurry-up Food

In every part of Rio de Janeiro, you'll find lunch-counter restaurants advertising *galetos* – spring chickens barbecued over charcoal. They make fast, cheap and often delicious meals.

Stand-up snack bars, known as *lanchonetes*, are everywhere. They serve *lanches* – meaning 'snacks', not 'lunches'. These are the places to try Brazilian appetizers – such as codfish balls, chicken patties, shrimp pies or cheese patties.

A recent development is the proliferation of American-style hamburger and hot-dog emporia, clean and brash and very popular with young Brazilians. And for snacks on the run there are countless pushcarts dealing in sandwiches, hot dogs or popcorn.

On many a Rio street you'll find a lady from Bahia in her flowing dress, beads and white turban, sitting behind a tray of the richest but subtlest cookies and cakes imaginable. In a glass case beneath this she displays a small selection of snacks – often home-made from great recipes, such as *acarajé* and *vatapá*.

Desserts in restaurants or at snack bars can be overpoweringly

Fresh fruit juices are a healthful treat at inexpensive stand-up bars on street corners all over Rio.

sweet, probably thanks to a combination of the Portuguese influence and the early boom of the Brazilian sugar industry.

If such confections prove too much for your taste, switch to fresh fruit – which is varied and abundant, and generally a joy.

Tips on Service

There is no government tax on restaurant meals, but a 10 percent service charge is often added to the bill. If your waiter serves you well, then you may want to leave an additional 5 percent, or more, on the table.

The majority of Rio restaurants offer an optional *couvert* – often an overpriced dish of olives and pickled carrots, broccoli and cucumber, and a few quail eggs. Feel free to wave it away if you don't find it appealing.

On most Brazilian restaurant tables you'll find two shakers, one filled with salt and the other with toothpicks. If you want pepper, ask the waiter for *pimenta do reino*: you'll probably be served a whole tray of condiments.

When a restaurant is full, it is not customary to join a table of strangers – even if one person is occupying a table for four. You'll just have to wait for a free table.

Drinks

Brazil's most popular aperitif, the *caipirinha*, is similar to a Mexican margarita, but instead of tequila, the firewater is *cachaça*, distilled from sugar cane. Ice and lemon soften the blow of this potent concoction. A *batida* is a cocktail – usually whipped up in a blender – of *cachaça*, ice, sugar and fruit juice. Among favorite flavours are lemon, peach, coconut and passion fruit.

Brazilian wines enjoy less fame than they deserve. The best of them come from Rio Grande do Sul, in the mild southern part of the country. There are reds, whites and rosés to choose from. In hot weather, all wines tend to be served chilled.

Brazilian beer is a great national asset. It is always served very cold. Draft beer *(chope)* is the favourite, but some restaurants only serve bottled beer – which may come in large bottles.

After dinner many restaurants serve complimentary coffee. Or you can have a *cafezinho* at one of the coffee bars. You're expected to pour sugar into the little cup (capacity just over 2 fluid ounces) before the coffee is poured into it. Brazilians like their coffee very sweet, and very often.

To Help You Order…

Could we have a table?   **Queríamos uma mesa.**
I'd like a/an/some…   **Queria…**

beer	**uma cerveja**	milk	**leite**
bill (the)	**a conta**	mineral water	**uma água mineral**
bread	**pão**	napkin	**um guardanapo**
butter	**manteiga**	potatoes	**batatas**
coffee	**um café**	rice	**arroz**
dessert	**sobremesa**	salad	**uma salada**
fish	**peixe**	sandwich	**um sanduíche**
fruit	**fruta**	soup	**sopa**
ice cream	**um sorvete**	sugar	**açúcar**
meat	**carne**	tea	**chá**
menu (the)	**o cardápio**	wine	**vinho**

…and Read the Menu

abacaxi	pineapple	**framboesas**	raspberries
alho	garlic	**frango**	chicken
almôndegas	meatballs	**frito**	fried
arroz	rice	**goiaba**	guava
assado	roasted	**grelhado**	grilled
azeitonas	olives	**lagosta**	spiny lobster
bacalhau	cod	**laranja**	orange
badejo	sea bass	**legumes**	vegetables
bife	beefsteak	**limão**	lemon
bolo	cake	**maçã**	apple
cabrito	kid	**melancia**	watermelon
camarão	shrimp	**morangos**	strawberries
caranguejo	crab	**ovo**	egg
carneiro	lamb	**peixe**	fish
cavala	mackerel	**pescadinha**	whiting
chouriço	a spicy sausage	**pimentão**	green pepper
costeletas	pork ribs	**queijo**	cheese
dobrada	tripe	**siri**	beach crab
enguias	eel	**sobremesa**	dessert
feijão	beans	**sorvete**	ice cream
fígado	liver	**uva**	grapes
flan	caramel custard	**vitela**	veal

BLUEPRINT for a Perfect Trip

How to Get There

Although the fares and conditions described below have all been carefully checked, it is advisable to consult a travel agent for the latest information on fares and other arrangements.

From North America

BY AIR: There are daily nonstop flights to Rio from Los Angeles, Miami, New York and San Francisco, with nonstop flights from Toronto four times a week and from Montreal once a week. Travelers can connect to these flights from over 50 cities in the U.S.A. and Canada.

There are a number of promotional fares currently available. One is the Super-APEX fare offered by the major carriers. Passengers must book both arrival and departure dates 14 days before departure. The minimum stay is 21 days, the maximum 90. Children under 12 fly for 75%.

Charter Flights and Package Tours: Tour operators are now offering seven-night packages to Rio from several major cities, including flights, transfers, accommodation and some meals. Rio is also featured on tours of from 12 to 30 days that include other major Latin American cities.

From Great Britain

BY AIR: There are nonstop flights from Heathrow or Gatwick to Rio most days of the week. Direct flying time averages 10 to 11 hours. First Class, Business and Economy fares are available. The Point-to-Point fare offers a 30% reduction for a minimum 13-day to a maximum 90-day stay.

Charter Flights and Package Tours: Charter flights take off from London once a week or more, depending on demand. Fares tend to be higher from June through September. Rio is also a favorite stop on flying tours of the South American capitals. No fly/drive packages are offered, but car rental can be arranged upon arrival at the airport.

Brazil Air Pass: The Brazil Air Pass – developed by Embratur, the government tourism authority – may be purchased, only outside the country, at travel agencies in North America and Europe. In Brazil, passengers cash in the pass for domestic-airline tickets tracing whatever route they wish, using the same airline (provided the same sector is not flown more than once in the same direction) up to a total of 5 flights. There is a flat rate for each additional flight. This Air Pass is good for 21 days.

BY SEA: A number of cruises from Southampton to South America include Rio as a port of call. Some cruise operators fly tourists out to Rio to join a ship, with at least a two-day stopover in the city.

When to Go

Everybody wants to join in Rio's Carnival, which falls in February or early March. But it's not really the best time of year for a visit: hotels are overflowing and Carioca efficiency wilts. It's also the Brazilian summer and rainy season, and temperatures can reach 90° or 95° Fahrenheit every day for weeks at a time. To beat the crowds (if not the heat), come to Rio a few weeks before Carnival. The pre-holiday festivities are lively in themselves.

The driest months of the year are May through October (the South American winter), a time when the temperature is lower and you may actually see some sweaters. Another bonus: Rio's cultural scene is much more active at this time of year.

The following chart will help you predict Rio's weather:

		J	F	M	A	M	J	J	A	S	O	N	D
Temperature	°C	26	26	25	24	22	21	21	21	22	22	23	24
	°F	85	85	80	75	72	70	70	70	72	72	74	75
Days of rain		13	12	12	11	9	7	7	7	9	13	13	15

While You're in Brazil…

It's a big country – as big as all of Europe. While you're there, you can see much more of it if you have a Brazil Air Pass (see p. 103). Here are some cities you can easily visit by air – or by luxurious long-distance bus:

São Paulo, the financial and commercial capital of Brazil, goes straight up – from the loftiest palm trees to the tops of the soaring skyscrapers. It's a bit like New York City gone mad, a riot of concrete, glass, superhighways and smog. São Paulo is somewhat cooler than Rio, permitting a faster pace of life. With a population above 12 million, South America's biggest city is a cosmopolitan center, with nearly a thousand restaurants of many nationalities, and sophisticated nightlife.

Salvador (the capital of Bahia) is the place for history, folklore, and enough perfect beaches to accommodate just about the entire population of Brazil. Founded by Tomé de Sousa in 1549, Salvador defends its position as the cradle of Brazilian civilization. Colonial mansions and Baroque churches decorated with ornate gold leaf coexist with holiday hotels and shanty-town huts. In Salvador, religion is a way of life: Roman Catholic Masses are said alongside mystic *candomblé* rituals, Christian saints are mixed up with African gods … and everything against the background of a permanent carnival atmosphere.

Recife claims the title 'Venice of Brazil'. But the resemblance ends with the bridges, waterways and Baroque churches, for Recife, the capital of Pernambuco state, is a lively, brash, modern city of over one million. Ornate 17th- and 18th-century churches, old colonial houses, and ancient forts and monasteries are set in the luminous green of a luxuriant tropical vegetation. Another top attraction is the dazzling six-mile-long beach. Only a few miles away, Recife's sister city, Olinda, is a national monument, a time capsule of colonial Brazil.

Belém. Just south of the Equator, Belém (Portuguese for Bethlehem) stands, hot, humid and sultry, on the threshold of the Amazon basin. Its back garden contains more than 18,000 species of plants. Belém's skyscrapers loom awkwardly over trim colonial buildings of slightly faded splendor. Its tropical temperament matches the climate, and businessmen regularly fix appointments for 'before' or 'after' the daily deluge.

An A–Z Summary of Practical Information and Facts

A   **ACCOMMODATION.** Most of the year, Rio's 20,000 hotel rooms meet the demand, but at Carnival time some 300,000 or 400,000 tourists roll into town. Of the overflow, the lucky ones stay with friends or go to agencies specializing in 'holiday rentals' of furnished apartments. Others are reduced to signing in at 'high-turnover' motels on the outskirts of town that normally rent rooms by the hour to anonymous couples. Moral: don't go to Rio at Carnival time without a confirmed hotel reservation.

Embratur, the national tourism authority, classifies hotels from one to five stars in ascending order of luxury. Breakfast is normally included in the price of the room. In small inexpensive hotels, a clear distinction is made between *quarto*, meaning a room with a toilet and basin, and *apartamento*, a room with a separate bathroom. The Passaporte Brazil, available at travel agencies all over the country, gives considerable discounts on hotels, entertainment, domestic air fares and excursions.

I'd like a single/double room.	**Queria um quarto de solteiro/ de casal.**
with toilet	**com banheiro**
with bath/shower	**com banheira/chuveiro**
What's the daily rate?	**Qual é o preço da diária?**

AIRPORTS. Aeroporto do Galeão – the international airport of Rio de Janeiro – has all the usual facilities and conveniences, including a shopping and service center. It even has an inbound duty-free shop for arriving passengers (Payment in Brazilian currency is not accepted.)

Arriving in Rio, you have the choice of 'red' or 'green' channels in the customs hall. If you have 'nothing to declare', go through the 'green' aisle, where you will be asked to press a button which shows a green or red light. If you get the red light, your baggage is searched.

Just beyond the customs hall is an information desk operated by Riotur, Rio de Janeiro's official tourist agency, where multilingual receptionists answer questions, distribute pamphlets and even help with hotel reservations. Opposite is a bank for changing some money into Cruzeiros.

On either side of the Riotur counter are the desks of authorized taxi companies, which charge standard fares from the airport according to destination; you pay on the spot in advance and give the receipt to the driver. The trip to the business center takes 30 to 40 minutes, to the beach zone up to an hour. Ordinary taxis are also available, but foreigners who have no idea of the proper fee should make inquiries about fares before using them. A much cheaper way to reach central Rio is by bus. Convenient air-conditioned buses connect both the international airport and Santos Dumont airport in the city. Another bus line goes right along the beaches to and from the international airport (the destination sign says 'Galeão').

Outbound passengers should check in 90 minutes ahead of time for international flights (1 hour for domestic). An airport departure tax is levied.

Santos Dumont Airport is so close to the center of town that a businessman could walk from his office to his private jet. Apart from small private planes, the jets of the air-bridge service between Rio and São Paulo (see TRANSPORTATION) use Santos Dumont. All other domestic services operate from the international airport.

To reach Santos Dumont from the Zona Sul resorts, you can take any of the air-conditioned buses going to the center of Rio, and you will be let off within easy walking distance of the airport.

BICYCLES *(bicicleta).* On the car-free island of Paquetá bikes are a popular form of transportation, along with double-bikes (two bikes attached side by side) and tandems. There is a new cycle track along the beach from Recreio dos Bandeirante to Leme, and beach roads are closed to traffic (except bikes) on Sundays and holidays. Bikes can be hired in many of the major hotels near the beach, e.g. Hotel Rio Othon, Av. Atlântica, 3264. Rates vary.

CAMPING. There are large campsites at Barra da Tijuca and Recreio dos Bandeirantes. Members of the Camping Club of Brazil (for address, see below) and travelers with an international camping card pay around half the price of non-members. For a complete list of campsites in Brazil, with local maps and details of facilities and travel connections, consult one of the an-

C nual camping guides *(Agenda CCB)* available from the Camping Club-Camping Clube do Brasil, Rua Senador Dantas, 75, 29th floor; tel. 210 3171. Don't be tempted to use beaches as impromptu campsites. Lonely beaches attract all manner of criminals, some of them violent.

CAR RENTAL and DRIVING. International and local car-rental agencies have offices at the airports, in the business center, and in Copacabana, Ipanema, Leblon and other tourist areas. Some companies will only rent cars to drivers over 25 with valid licenses held for at least one year. Normally third-party insurance is included in the charge, but collision insurance is a sizable extra. A federal tax of 5% is added to the bill.

Driving in Rio. All you need to drive in Rio is strong nerves. The local drivers are not noted for their courtesy; nor are they fanatical about obeying signals and laws. Even bus drivers sometimes run red lights, especially late at night, if they're in a hurry and no other traffic is visible. Cars may pass you on either side. If you miss a turn-off, take the road marked 'Retorno' (Return), for a second try at it. Pedestrians need to be extremely cautious: they have the lowest priority in the scheme of things in Rio.

The laws, insofar as they are observed, follow normal international practice. The speed limit is 80 kilometers per hour (50 mph) on all highways, including expressways, 60 kph (37 mph) in towns.

Parking is so difficult, especially in the beach areas, that illegal triple parking in the street is quite common. Rio has no parking meters, but some areas have parking wardens *(guardadores autônomous)* who legally collect a posted fee for two hours of parking. Elsewhere, neighborhood children or old men often supervise parking, expecting a fee for watching over the car. A car wash is sometimes part of the deal. Hotel parking, in guarded areas, can be comparatively expensive. Use a steering lock if you leave your car – otherwise it might disappear. The same thing can happen if you park illegally, although this time it will probably be in the police pound.

Service stations are usually open at night and on Sundays. Make sure that the service-station attendant sets the fuel meter back at zero before filling your tank and uses the correct fuel. Many cars in Brazil run on alcohol-based fuel. To change gallons into liters, see chart on p. 113.

Repairs. The car-rental agency collects and replaces any car that breaks down. In an emergency, dial the police – 190.

Signs. The streets of Rio are very well identified, with illuminated blue-and-white signs on the street corners. Don't worry about those apparent mystery streets *Placa Original em Conserto* and *PlacaOriginal Danificada* – they mean the sign is being fixed.

Some road signs:

Cruzamento	Crossroads
Curva perigosa	Dangerous curve
Descida íngreme	Steep hill
Desvio	Detour
Devagar	Slow
Encruzilhada	Crossroads
Estacionamento proibido	No parking
Homens na pista	Men working
Mão dupla	Two-way traffic
Mantenha sua direita/esquerda	Keep right/left
Obras	Men working
Ônibus	Bus stop
Pare	Stop
Pedágio	Toll booth
Pedestres	Pedestrians
Perigo	Danger
Posto de emergência	First-aid post
Proibida a entrada	No entry
Saída de caminhões	Truck (Lorry) exit
Veículos pesados	Heavy vehicles

I'd like to rent a car today/tomorrow.	**Queria alugar um carro para hoje/amanhã.**
for one day/a week	**por um dia/uma semana**
Please include full insurance.	**Que inclua um seguro contra todos os riscos, por favor.**
Fill the tank with gas (petrol)/ alcohol, please.	**Encha o tanque de gasolina/ alcool, por favor.**

C   Check the oil/tires/battery.   **Verifique o óleo/os pneus/a bateria,**
                                             por favor.

I've had a breakdown.   **O meu carro está quebrado.**
There's been an accident.   **Houve um acidente.**

CHILDREN. Cariocas take their babies to the beach before they can walk
or talk, so children of any age will have plenty of company. Be sure to keep
a close eye on your offspring at the ocean beaches, where tides can be dangerous. And don't let an overdose of sun spoil the whole vacation. For
other things to do, there's always the zoo. The Botanical Garden is outstanding, and most children want to have a look at the model airplanes flying in Parque do Flamengo.

Hotels routinely arrange babysitting services for their guests. It's wise
to organize this a day in advance if possible, especially for weekend services. You can also find reputable services listed in the 'Cidade' (City)
pull-out section of the daily newspaper *Jornal do Brasil.*

Lost children – who are treated with great understanding by Cariocas,
including the police – usually turn up at the nearest police precinct. On the
beach, check the nearest lifeguard station.

Can you get me a babysitter for   **Pode me arrumar uma babá para**
tonight?   **esta noite?**

CLOTHING. The relaxed informality may surprise travelers from conser-
vative countries where bathing suits, or even shorts, would be unthinkable
in a restaurant or store. Too-casual or shirtless patrons are occasionally
barred from some restaurants, and a certain degree of modesty is called for
when visiting historic churches.

If you visit Rio in its summertime (the northern hemisphere's winter),
you'll probably need an umbrella sometimes. The locals rarely wear rain-
coats because they're too hot. It's also easy to escape the rain by walking
under the projecting balconies or arcades common to most buildings. In
Rio's winter (the northern hemisphere's summer) pack a sweater.

Buying swimsuits and sports clothes is a popular tourist pastime in
fashionable Rio, even though the numbering of sizes can be somewhat
confusing. The obvious solution is to try everything on.

110 Can I try it on?   **Posso esperimentá-lo?**

COMMUNICATIONS

Post offices are found all over town: look for the yellow sign 'ECT' – for Empresa Brasileira de Correios e Telégrafos. The post office at Rio de Janeiro international airport is open 24 hours a day. Branch offices tend to work 8 am to 6 or 8 pm, Monday through Friday; 9-11 am on Saturdays.

General Delivery (Posta Restante). If you don't know ahead of time where you'll be staying, you can have mail addressed to you *Posta Restante* and pick it up at the appropriate window in the main post office in Rua Primeiro de Março, 64.

American Express also does a lively, if profitless, business in general-delivery mail at its representative office in Copacabana. Card holders or travelers possessing the company's checks may have mail addressed:

c/o Kontik Franstur, Avenida Atlântica, 2316A, cep 22041 Copacabana, Rio de Janeiro, Brazil

Don't give your mail to a hotel porter to post; sad stories are told of tourists charged airmail rates for postcards sent by sea, if at all. A recent innovation in Brazil is the yellow street-corner mailbox. Mail is collected irregularly.

Telegrams, telex. All post offices accept telegrams. The larger offices have telex and fax facilities, too. For tourists, the most convenient is probably upstairs at Avenida N. S. de Copacabana, 540A (open 8 am to 8 pm daily).

To phone in a telegram, dial 135.

Telephone. The international service, using satellites and other advanced equipment, works extremely well. Public telephones are placed in large protective domes, commonly called *orelhões* – 'big ears'. Orange ones are for local calls, blue ones (with 'DDD' on) for long-distance. Tokens *(ficha)* are sold at most newsstands, individually or in strips. Ask for *Local* tokens if you're ringing a Rio number, and *DDD* tokens if the call is further afield (but you can't dial out of Brazil from a street telephone).

For long-distance calls, phone 101; for overseas calls, phone 000111.

Hotels in Rio tend to let their guests make local calls free, but add a service charge to the tariff for international calls. At the airports and several other key locations, there are public telephone offices where you can make long-distance and overseas calls. The one on Avenida N. S. de Copacabana, 462, **111**

C is open day and night. Although you'll probably decide not to carry much money around as a security measure, if you phone abroad from a public telephone office you'll have to leave a sizable deposit – in Cruzeiros.

Have you received any mail for…?	**Chegou correspondência para …?**
I'd like a stamp for this letter/ this postcard.	**Quero um selo para esta carta/ este postal, por favor.**
special delivery (express)	**expresso**
airmail/registered	**via aérea/registrado**
I want to send a telegram to…	**Quero mandar um telegrama para ..**
Give me …*fichas*, please.	**Dê-me … fichas, por favor.**
Can you get me this number in …?	**Pode ligar-me para este número em …**
collect (reverse-charge) call	**a cobrar**
person-to-person (personal) call	**pessoa a pessoa**

COMPLAINTS. If you have a grievance about bad service or overcharging at a hotel, restaurant or shop, it makes sense to try to work things out with the manager. But if this fails, take your complaint – along with any pertinent documents – to the municipal tourist office: Riotur, Rua da Assembléia 10, 9th floor; tel. 242-8000.

CONSULATES *(consulado).*More than 50 consulates and commercial missions operate in the former capital. Most embassies are now based in Brasilia.

Australia	Rua Voluntários da Patria 45, Sala 204, tel. 286-7922
Canada	Rua Lauro Müller 116, Sala 1104, Botafogo, tel. 275-2137
Eire	Av. Princesa Isabel 323, Copacabana; tel. 275-0196
Great Britain	Praia do Flamengo, 284, 2nd floor; tel. 542-1422
South Africa	Rua Lauro Müller 116, Sala 1107, Botafogo; tel. 542-6191
112 U.S.A.	Avenida Presidente Wilson, 147; tel. 292-7117

CONVERTER CHARTS. Brazil uses the metric system.

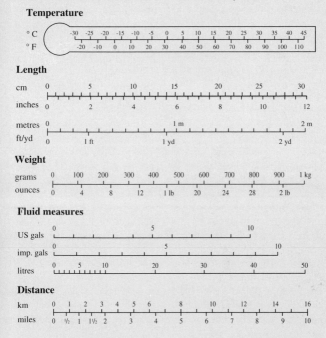

Temperature

| °C | -30 -25 -20 -15 -10 -5 0 5 10 15 20 25 30 35 40 45 |
| °F | -20 -10 0 10 20 30 40 50 60 70 80 90 100 110 |

Length

| cm | 0 5 10 15 20 25 30 |
| inches | 0 2 4 6 8 10 12 |

| metres | 0 1 m 2 m |
| ft/yd | 0 1 ft 1 yd 2 yd |

Weight

| grams | 0 100 200 300 400 500 600 700 800 900 1 kg |
| ounces | 0 4 8 12 1 lb 20 24 28 2 lb |

Fluid measures

US gals	0 5 10
imp. gals	0 5 10
litres	0 5 10 20 30 40 50

Distance

| km | 0 1 2 3 4 5 6 8 10 12 14 16 |
| miles | 0 ½ 1 1½ 2 3 4 5 6 7 8 9 10 |

CRIME and THEFT. Crime in Rio is a very real problem, and precautions should not be disregarded. Always store your valuables in the hotel's safe. Take nothing of value to the beach, where 'beach rats' (see p. 44) are brilliant at stealing the belongings of careless or unwary tourists. Beware of pickpockets in crowds. Stay clear of lonely beaches and unlit streets. Avoid displays of jewelry or elegant clothing.Note that possession of even small quantities of drugs can bring up to two years' imprisonment; the authorities make little distinction between marijuana, pills and hard drugs.

I want to report a theft. **Quero denunciar um roubo**. 113

C   **CUSTOMS** *(alfândega)* **and ENTRY REGULATIONS**. Canadian, British and Irish nationals and citizens of most Commonwealth countries need only a valid passport to enter Brazil, while visitors from Australia, New Zealand, South Africa and the U.S. require a visa.

No vaccinations are required unless you are arriving from or have recently visited countries infected with certain serious diseases (cholera, yellow fever, etc.). In case of doubt, consult a travel agent well in advance of your departure date. The following chart shows the duty-free items you may take into Brazil and, when returning home, into your own country:

Into	Cigarettes		Cigars		Tobacco	Spirits		Wine
Brazil*	400	and	25	and	250g		2l	
Australia	250	or	250g	or	250g	1l	or	1l
Canada	200	and	50	and	900g	1.1l	or	1.1l
Eire	200	or	50	or	250g	1l	and	2l
N. Zealand	200	or	50	or	250g	1.1l	and	4.5l
S.Africa	400	and	50	and	250g	1l	and	2l
U.K.	200	or	50	or	250g	1l	and	2l
U.S.A	200	and	100	and	**	1l	or	1l

* International passengers may purchase duty-free goods for a total of U.S.$300 or the equivalent in another currency on arrival in Brazil, including a restricted amount of alcoholic beverages.

** A reasonable quantity.

Currency restrictions. A non-resident may import an unlimited amount of foreign currency and traveler's checks and a reasonable amount of Brazilian Cruzeiros. The amount exported cannot be greater than the sum brought into the country, minus the funds spent while in Brazil.

E   **ELECTRIC CURRENT** *(corrente elétrica)*. In most places in Rio the current is 110-volt, 60 cycles (the same as in the United States). However, some hotels have 220-volt outlets; they are usually marked.

I need an adaptor/a battery.   **Preciso de um adaptador/uma pilha, por favor.**

EMERGENCIES. Depending on the problem, refer to the separate entries in this section (CONSULATES, HEALTH AND MEDICAL CARE, POLICE). Hotel staff will be your greatest immediate help.

Here are the 24-hour telephone numbers for emergency use:

Police	190
Fire	193
Ambulance	192

GUIDES. All hotels and travel agencies can provide you with pamphlets from licensed excursion companies offering guided tours in Rio and far-ther afield. The guides, normally well briefed on local history, folklore and nature, generally speak several foreign languages, including English.

We'd like an English-speaking guide. **Queremos um guia que fale inglês.**

HAIRDRESSERS *(cabeleireiro)* **and BARBERS** *(barbeiro)*. As you'd expect, the shops in five-star hotels charge much more than neighborhood salons. You should tip the hairdresser at least 10%.

The following vocabulary will help:

I'd like a shampoo and set.	**Queria um shampoo e penteado.**
haircut	**um corte**
blow-dry (brushing)	**uma escova**
permanent wave	**uma permanente**
color rinse	**uma rinsagem**
manicure	**uma manicure**
Don't cut it too short.	**Não corte muito curto.**
A little more off (here).	**Corte mais um pouco (aqui).**

HEALTH and MEDICAL CARE. Medical insurance to cover illness or accident while abroad is an investment you should consider. Your travel agent or insurance company will have modestly priced policies available.

Although a risk of malaria exists in certain parts of Brazil, a vacation in Rio holds no special health hazards. You should avoid the tap water, how-ever, and take care that an overdose of sun on the first few days doesn't spoil the rest of your vacation. It's also wise to go easy on food and drink until you get over your jet lag.

Hotels usually have the names of doctors who speak English (or French, German or Spanish); you can also ask your consulate for a list. Or consult the Rio Health Collective, tel. 325-9300, ext. 44.

Municipal hospitals with round-the-clock emergency rooms include:

Miguel Couto, Rua Bartolomeu Mitre 1108 (Leblon); tel. 274–2121
Rocha Maia, Rua General Severiano, 91 (Botafogo); tel. 295–2121
Souza Aguiar, Praça da República, 111 (enter); tel. 221–2121

Pharmacies and drug stores are found in abundance in all parts of Rio. *Drogarias* sell, among other things, many familiar patent medicines, but only *farmácias* are allowed to make up prescriptions and give injections. Several *farmácias* have a policy of staying open round the clock, seven days a week. Your hotel or taxi driver will know the location of one near you. Otherwise, check the 'Cidade' (City) section of the *Jornal do Brasil*.

Where's the nearest (all-night) pharmacy?	**Onde fica a farmácia (de plantão) mais próxima?**
I need a doctor/dentist.	**Preciso de um médico/dentista.**
an ambulance	**uma ambuluância**
hospital	**hospital**
sunburn	**queimadura de sol**
sunstroke	**uma insolação**
a fever	**febre**
stomach ache	**dôr de estômago**

HITCHHIKING. There's no law against it, but hitchhiking can be dangerous in Brazil, as elsewhere.

HOURS (see also under COMMUNICATIONS and MONEY MATTERS). Many offices and shops have opening and closing hours that defy categorization. They are, to say the least, erratic and unpredictable.

Government offices are usually open 8 am to 5 pm Monday to Friday. But some open as late as 11 am and close a bit later in the afternoon.

Shops and stores are generally open at least from 9 am to 6 pm, but in certain neighborhoods they function much longer hours, sometimes opening before 8 am and closing around 10 pm. Some local food stores open Sunday mornings.

Museums tend to close on Mondays. Their weekday hours are from noon or 2 pm to 5 or 6 pm; weekends they open briefly from 2 or 3 pm and close at 5 or 6 pm.

LANGUAGE. Don't forget that the language of Brazil is Portuguese, not Spanish. If you say *gracias* instead of *obrigado* to a Carioca, it's like saying 'thanks' instead of *merci* in Quebec; in effect, you're announcing that you're lumping everybody in South America into the same bag and don't care about local sensibilities – which is no way to make friends.

The slangy version of Portuguese spoken in Rio is nasal, but with a musical intonation. Though it's easier to understand than the language of Portugal, most foreigners still find it extremely difficult – but if you learn a few words, the gesture is much appreciated. Your high-school Spanish will help you understand signs and menus; and in a pinch most Brazilians innately understand Spanish. The most widely spoken foreign language is English. Well-educated people are often fluent in French or German, too.

The Berlitz PORTUGUESE PHRASE BOOK AND DICTIONARY covers most of the situations you're likely to encounter in Rio, as it gives the Brazilian expressions whenever they differ from the ones used in Portugal. Also useful is the Portuguese-English/English-Portuguese pocket dictionary, which has a special menu-reader supplement. A few words to get you going:

Good morning/Good evening	**Bom dia/Boa noite**
Please	**Por favor**
Thank you	**Obrigado/Obrigada** (fem.)
Good-bye	**Adeus**
Yes/No	**Sim/Não**
Do you speak English?	**Fala inglês?**
I don't speak Portuguese.	**Não falo português.**

LAUNDRY and DRY CLEANING *(lavanderia; tinturaria)*. Hotel laundry service is fast. In small hotels the room maids sometimes do the job themselves in their spare time. Self-service laundries are a very recent innovation in Rio; two or three have opened in Copacabana. A few are already listed in the yellow pages of the telephone directory under

L   'Lavanderias'. Dry cleaners are located all over town, offering two-day service.

LOST and FOUND. Start tracing any lost property at your hotel reception desk; the personnel will know the proper procedures and addresses. For lost documents, the postal service has an office (open 8 am–6 pm) at:

Rua Primeiro de Março, 64; 1st floor; tel. 159

If you left your property in the subway, try the *Achados e Perdidos* ('found and lost') office at the Cinelândia *metrô* stop by Pedro Lessa, open Monday to Friday, from 10 am to 1 pm and from 2 pm to 6 pm. If you've lost something in a taxi, try the taxi drivers' union at:

Rua Santana, 77, 2nd floor; tel. 221–6662

I've lost my wallet/purse (handbag)/my passport.	**Perdi a minha carteira/bolsa/ o meu passaporte.**

M   **MAPS.** The free pamphlets distributed to tourists contain simple maps of Rio. More detailed maps are sold at newsstands. A relatively inexpensive but useful *Mapa Turístico* is published annually by Geomapas. The easiest map to read is the one included in the *Quatro Rodas* magazine's *Guia do Rio*, also available at newsstands. The guide itself lists hotels, sightseeing attractions, bus routes etc., and describes and evaluates hundreds of Rio restaurants.

The maps in this book were prepared by Falk-Verlag, Hamburg, which also publishes a complete map of Rio de Janeiro.

I'd like a street map of Rio.	**Queria um mapa do Rio.**

MEETING PEOPLE. The Cariocas are relaxed, friendly people who are easy to get to know. Since they are as keen on getting suntanned as any tourist, the beach is the logical place to make new friends. Some outdoor cafés also have an atmosphere conducive to meeting people.

The languid pace typical of the tropics is very evident in Rio, sometimes frustratingly so. But nothing is gained by raising your voice or losing your patience. Instead, try to slow down and put things into perspective.

How do you do?   **Muito prazer.**

How are you?	**Como está?**	**M**
Very well, thank you.	**Muito bem,**	
	obrigado/obrigada (fem.)	

MONEY MATTERS

Currency. In an attempt to halt the vertiginous inflation in Brazil, the government has decided to make the Brazilian curency equivalent to a strong monetary unit – the US$. A new monetary unit, the Real (R$) is currently being brought into circulation, and corresponds roughly to the US$. Notes available in this currency are R$1, 5, 10, 50, 100.

For currency restrictions, see CUSTOMS AND ENTRY REGULATIONS.

Currency exchange. There are two rates of exchange: the official bank one and the 'parallel', the going rate in the street, which is usually 20 to 25 per cent better and is given at travel agencies and currency exchange offices *(câmbio)*. Since it changes from day to day you'll find it useful to buy a little at a time. You can check the parallel rate on the front page of the *Jornal do Brasil*. Your hotel can change money, probably at a better rate than the bank's but still appreciably worse than the parallel market's. Currency can be changed during the week at all banks – the hours are from 10 am to 4.30 pm, Monday to Friday – as well as at currency exchange offices *(câmbio)* – open from 8 am to 6 pm, Monday to Friday. Major hotels and some restaurants can change money on weekends and holidays.

Traveler's checks. It is certainly safer to hold your holiday funds in checks, which can be reclaimed if lost, rather than in cash. However, if you do have dollars, and keep them in your hotel safe, you'll find they attract a better rate. It's a good idea to follow instructions given for recording where and when you cashed each check.

Credit cards. Major hotels, restaurants, stores and car-rental agencies accept the major credit cards.

I want to change some dollars/ pounds.	**Queria trocar dólares/libras.**
Can you cash a traveler's check?	**Pode trocar um cheque de viagem?**
Can I pay with this credit card?	**Posso pagar com este cartão de crédito?**

119

N **NEWSPAPERS and MAGAZINES** *(jornal; revista)*. Entertainment listings are found in the Portuguese-language dailies, notably *Jornal do Brasil* and *O Globo*. For more-comprehensive news coverage you can buy the *International Herald Tribune* (edited in Paris and printed via satellite in Miami), which is on sale in certain hotels and at principal newsstands. Because of shipping expenses, it costs many times the price of local papers.

Time and *Newsweek* are sold every week on almost all Rio newsstands. Bookstores and selected newsstands sell many other American, British and European magazines, as well.

P **PHOTOGRAPHY.** Well-known brands of film are sold in Rio – but at prices considerably higher than you'd expect, so it's wise to stock up before you leave home. Processing in Rio is good but expensive.

You are not allowed to take pictures of military installations. In Brazil, this seems to include the toll booths *(pedagios)* of expressways.

Usually, airport X-ray machines do not ruin film – but to be on the safe side, put your films in a bag to be examined separately by the checkers.

I'd like a roll of film for this camera.	**Quero um filme para esta máquina.**
black-and-white film	**um filme preto e branco**
a color film	**um filme a cores**
color-slide film	**um filme de slides**
35-mm film	**um filme de trinta e cinco milimétros**
How long will it take to develop this film?	**Quanto tempo leva para revelar este filme?**
May I take a picture?	**Posso tirar uma fotografia?**

POLICE *(policia)*. The police you'll see in Rio, although they have the duties of municipal police, are members of the Military Police force (*Policia militar* – PM). The civilian police take care of judicial matters and carry out investigations. Crimes should be reported to the civilian police. The police are patient and courteous with foreigners. If you have a problem, go to one of the many blue-and-white octagonal police posts (marked PM-RIO) that are located at central points.

The emergency telephone number for the police is 190.

PUBLIC HOLIDAYS *(feriado).*

Jan 1	*Dia de Confraternização Universal*	Universal Brotherhood Day
Jan 20	*Dia de São Sebastião*	St Sebastian's Day (local holiday, Rio)
April 21	*Tiradentes*	Tiradentes' Day (martyr of independence)
May 1	*Dia do Trabalho*	Labor Day
Sept 7	*Independência do Brasil*	Independence Day
Oct 12	*Nossa Senhora de Aparecida*	Our Lady of Aparecida Day
Nov 2	*Finados*	All Souls' Day
Nov 15	*Proclamação da República*	Republic Day
Dec 8	*Imaculada Conceição**	Immaculate Conception*
Dec 25	*Natal*	Christmas Day
Movable dates:	*Terça-feira de Carnaval* *Sexta-feira da Paixão* *Corpus Christi*	Shrove Tuesday Good Friday Corpus Christi

* Religious holiday not necessarily affecting business life.
National holidays falling on weekends are moved to the nearest Monday.

RADIO and TV *(rádio; televisão).* Seven television channels can be watched in Rio de Janeiro. Some hotels receive TV broadcasts from the U.S. by satellite. Many radio stations broadcast from Rio on AM, FM and shortwave bands. There are no special programs for foreign tourists. To keep up with the news in North America or the U.K., you'll need a short-wave radio to pick up the Voice of America, Radio Canada International or the BBC. Several other foreign stations can be heard at night in Rio, too.

RELIGIOUS SERVICES. Brazil is the country with the largest Roman Catholic population in the world, but many other religions are active as well. In Rio de Janeiro there are services in a number of foreign languages, including English, French, German, Swedish and Chinese. The monthly **121**

booklets issued by the municipal tourism organization, Riotur, list times and places for these and other Catholic, Protestant and Jewish services.

TIME DIFFERENCES. Rio Standard Time is GMT minus three hours. During Brazilian summer (November–February), the clock is advanced one hour.

	L.A.	N.Y.	**Rio**	London	Sydney
January:	6 am	9 am	**noon**	2 pm	1 am
July:	8 am	11 am	**noon**	4 pm	1 am

TIPPING. Brazilians are not great tippers, since service is generally included. However, in top-class restaurants a 10% tip does not go amiss, while in simpler establishments the best course is to round off the sum. The same, essentially, goes for taxis. As for bellboys running errands, the odd coin is appropriate. Some further guidelines, in dollar equivalents:

Hotel porter, per bag	U.S. $2
Maid, per week	U.S. $10
Lavatory attendant	U.S. $1
Waiter	10%
Taxi driver	round up U.S. 50 cents
Hairdresser/Barber	U.S. $3–4
Tour guide	U.S. $3–5

TOILETS. Public conveniences are rare in Rio, but you can always find facilities in hotels, restaurants and bars. If there's an attendant on duty, a tip is expected (see above). 'Ladies' is *Senhoras* ; 'Gentlemen' is *Homens* or, sometimes, *Cavalheiros*. Signs are often abbreviated 'S' and 'H' (you might try remembering 'She' and 'He').

Where are the toilets? **Onde ficam os toiletes?**

TOURIST INFORMATION OFFICES. For information about Brazil, contact your nearest Brazilian consulate. For tourist information once you have arrived in Brazil, there is an array of official bodies to be approached.

Embratur, the national tourism authority, has an office at:
Rua Mariz e Barros, 13; tel. 273–2212

Turisrio, covering the State of Rio de Janeiro, is at:
Rua da Assembléia 10, 7th floor; tel. 252–4512

Riotur, the municipal tourism organization, has its headquarters at:
Rua da Assembléia 10, 8–9th floor; tel. 242–8000

For tourist information by telephone, try 264–8000; multilingual operators are on duty 24 hours a day.

Pamphlets and information can be obtained at the international airport (398–4073, 5 am–11 pm) and at any of these tourist information stands:

Sugar Loaf (at the cable-car station): open 8 am to 10 pm; tel. 541-3737
Marina da Gloria, Aterro do Flamengo (205–6447): open 8 am–5 pm.
Novo Rio terminal (arrival section): open 6 am to midnight; tel. 291-5151

For documentation on any aspect of Brazilian tourism, the library of **Cebitur** *(Centre Brasileiro de Informação Turistica)* is located at Rua Mariz e Barros, 13; tel. 273–2212.

TRANSPORTATION
Buses. More than 6,000 city buses race through the streets of Rio de Janeiro when traffic permits; if the traffic is jammed, they race their engines in protest. (They have no horns to blow; they were removed from the buses to promote urban tranquility.) Most of the buses are operated by private companies. There are more than 400 routes – which might explain why no bus maps of Rio are available. A list of bus routes may be found in Guia 4 Rodas, Rio de Janeiro, at all new-stands. It's best to ask advice on which bus to catch, and where. Avoid rush hours (between 5 and 7 pm), don't travel by bus after dark, and beware of pickpockets at all times.

You enter a city bus through the rear door and leave at the front. A conductor sits near the rear door by a turnstile. There is generally a standard fare – higher for air-conditioned buses.

For luxury public transport, ride the *frescões* ('big cool ones') – the air-conditioned buses linking the beach areas with central Rio. The destination is posted in the right-hand front window – 'Castelo' is the most frequently **123** seen. On the journey into town, these buses go to the central Menezes Côrtes bus station near Praça XV. On the return trip, the destinations cover most of the beach communities from Leme to São Conrado and even beyond. The *frescões* pull over at any bus stop on a signal from a passenger or potential passenger. Enter the bus, take a ticket and choose a seat; the conductor will eventually come around to collect the fixed-price fare.

Subway (underground). Studies had been carried out since before World War I, but Rio's first subway *(metrô)* system didn't go into operation until 1979. Early in 1982 the entire 15-station Line One was completed, linking the north zone at Praça Saens Peña in Tijuca to the south zone at Botafogo. A special 'integration' system permits subway riders to transfer to buses at subway stations. A spur line (Line Two) links the Line One station at Estácio to Maracanã soccer stadium and the northern suburbs beyond. Rio's clean, safe, efficient subway runs from 6 am to 11 pm, Monday through Saturday (Line One–Line Two is open until 8 pm). Almost 400,000 people use the subway daily.

Tram. Only one trolley-car line still functions in Rio, and it's well worth the trouble for the nostalgia alone. The terminal is near Largo da Carioca, and the ancient cars cross the aqueduct high above the Lapa section on the way up to suburban Santa Teresa (see p. 35).

Taxi. Most of Rio's 15,000 taxis are yellow two-door Volkswagens, many with the front passenger seat removed to permit relatively easy access to the back seat. There are taxi ranks at the airports and at the ferry and train stations, but taxis generally cruise the streets looking for clients. Except in a rainstorm, the supply of taxis exceeds the demand. Since the meter is likely to be a vintage model, checking it is not much help. Ask the driver to show you the official conversion chart, which will explain why you are paying several times the amount shown.

Ferries. Every day 150,000 passengers ride the ferries between Rio de Janeiro and Niterói, a 20-minute voyage. Most of them are commuters, who ignore the sea breezes and inspiring views. The ferry costs less than the cheapest city bus. If you're rushed, spend ten times as much and ride the hydrofoil *(aerobarco)*, which skims across the bay in five minutes. The embarkation points for ferries and hydrofoils are at Praça XV.

Long-distance buses. Air-conditioned buses, some equipped as sleepers, link Rio with cities as distant as Belém and Buenos Aires. The Novo Rio bus terminal, center of all this exotic activity, is in the Santo Cristo district of northern Rio – convenient for the bus drivers but not necessarily for the passengers. There are very frequent buses to São Paulo.

Trains. The main suburban train station, Estação Dom Pedro II, is just off Avenida Presidente Vargas, the widest street in town. In principle, travel by train is not recommended: the journeys seem longer than by bus, prices are higher, and service is less reliable and less frequent – the only exception being the luxury trains, including sleepers, to São Paulo.

Air links. About every half hour from 6 am to 10 pm there's a jet flight from Rio's Santos Dumont airport to Congonhas airport near the center of São Paulo. Four Brazilian airlines pool their resources for this air-bridge (*ponte aérea*). You don't need a reservation but merely board the first plane out. Other air-bridge schemes, based at Rio's international airport (Galeão), operate frequent jet flights to Brasilia and Belo Horizonte.

The Brazil Air Pass – which can only be purchased abroad – is good for up to a total of 5 flights all over the country during a 21-day period (see also p. 103). Timetables and fares for internal flights are listed in the monthly magazine *Guia Aeronáutico*.

Where's the nearest bus stop?	**Onde fica a parada de ônibus mais próximal?**
I want a ticket to …	**Queria uma passagem para …**
one-way (single) round-trip (return)	**ida e volta**
first/second class	**primeira/segunda classe**
Where can I get a taxi?	**Onde posso encontrar um táxi?**
What's the fare to …?	**Quanto custa a corrida para …?**

WATER. Don't drink tap water anywhere in Brazil – unless your hotel specifically states that it supplies purified water. Bottled mineral water is available at all bars and restaurants, either carbonated (*com gás*) or plain (*sem gás*). Ice cubes in drinks are normally made of purified water.

I'd like a bottle of mineral water.	**Queria uma garrafa de água mineral.**

SOME USEFUL EXPRESSIONS

yes/no	**sim/não**
please/thank you	**Por favor/obrigado (obrigada)**
excuse me/you're welcome	**perdão/de nada**
where/when/how	**onde/quando/como**
how long/how far	**quanto tempo/a que distância**
yesterday/today/tomorrow	**ontem/hoje/amanhã**
day/week/month/year	**dia/semana/mês/ano**
left/right	**esquerda/direita**
good/bad	**bom/mau**
big/small	**grande/pequeno**
cheap/expensive	**barato/caro**
hot/cold	**quente/frio**
old/new	**velho/novo**
open/closed	**aberto/fechado**
up/down	**em cima/em baixo**
here/there	**aqui/ali**
free (vacant)/occupied	**livre/ocupado**
early/late	**cedo/tarde**
easy/difficult	**fácil/difícil**
Does anyone here speak English?	**Alguém fala inglês?**
What does this mean?	**Que quer dizer isto?**
I don't understand.	**Não compreendo.**
Please write it down.	**Escreva, por favor.**
Is there an admission charge?	**Paga-se entrada?**
Waiter!/Waitress!	**Garçon!/Moça!**
I'd like …	**Queria …/Quero …**
How much is that?	**Quanto custa isto?**
Have you something less expensive?	**Tem alguma coisa mais em conta?**
Just a minute.	**Um momento.**
What time is it?	**Que horas são?**
Help me, please.	**Ajude-me, por favor.**
Get a doctor, quickly.	**Chame um médico, depressa.**

Index

An asterisk (*) next to a page number indicates a map reference.

INDEX

128